T0208214

From
Messed Up
to
Grown Up

JEFF HARRELL

WESTBOW
PRESS®
A DIVISION OF THOMAS NELSON
& ZONDERVAN

Scripture taken from the New King James Version®. Copyright © 1982 by Thomas Nelson. Used by permission. All rights reserved.

This book is a work of non-fiction. Unless otherwise noted, the author and the publisher make no explicit guarantees as to the accuracy of the information contained in this book and in some cases, names of people and places have been altered to protect their privacy.

WestBow Press books may be ordered through booksellers or by contacting:

WestBow Press
A Division of Thomas Nelson & Zondervan
1663 Liberty Drive
Bloomington, IN 47403
www.westbowpress.com
1 (866) 928-1240

Because of the dynamic nature of the Internet, any web addresses or links contained in this book may have changed since publication and may no longer be valid. The views expressed in this work are solely those of the author and do not necessarily reflect the views of the publisher, and the publisher hereby disclaims any responsibility for them.

Any people depicted in stock imagery provided by Getty Images are models, and such images are being used for illustrative purposes only. Certain stock imagery © Getty Images.

ISBN: 978-1-9736-5929-7 (sc)
ISBN: 978-1-9736-5930-3 (hc)
ISBN: 978-1-9736-5928-0 (e)

Library of Congress Control Number: 2019904070

Print information available on the last page.

WestBow Press rev. date: 04/11/2019

Foreword

I have known Jeff Harrell for thirty-nine years. I have watched with amazement as God has led him on his journey. Years ago, I counseled this successful businessman, husband, father and Christian to write a book about true success.

Psalms 1 says of the righteous man, "...whatever he does shall prosper" (Psalm 1:3, NKJV). I have known many to succeed in business but fail in their family or in their spiritual life.

Jeff, remarkably, has succeeded on every level through strong faith, hard work, loving commitment, and the power to bounce back.

I love this wonderful book. Too often books may simply diagnose challenges yet fail to give concrete steps of action. Not so with this book. Here you find proven steps of action as you find God's best for your life. Jeff gives us the manual we need to lay hold of the abundant life at every level.

Clearly written, deeply challenging, and honestly shared, the book chronicles the life not perfect but well-lived.

I commend it to all who desire a godly proven approach to true successful living.

Dr. Ron Phillips
Pastor Emeritus
Abba's House
Chattanooga, TN

A Note from the Author

With all of my heart, I want to play an active role in the rebuilding of our nation's family infrastructure. I don't want or hope to see change; I intend to experience it first-hand. We as parents have a responsibility to step up to the plate, mentor our youth, and stop depending on the government, educational system, and clergy to raise our children. It is our responsibility. God gave us the awesome task of raising the children we *chose* to have.

My beautiful wife Andi and I are committed to inspire and encourage strong families—not perfect families, but families that value character, morality, faith, and quality of life. And now we're watching our kids raise their children to value the same principles. We are also privileged to be Sunday School teachers to young married couples with children at our church. We want to see every child get what they deserve. And we think every child deserves to have parents who make loving and caring for their children a life-long priority.

But I didn't write this book because I have it all together. There are plenty of parents that probably did better jobs than we did. I messed up a lot. I did most everything backwards and upside down from how a parenting book would tell you to do it. And though it's fun to laugh at some of those mistakes now, they were not very funny at the time. If it weren't for the endless patience of my wife and the guidance from my heavenly Father, I fear that my life wouldn't look anywhere near as fulfilling as it does and is now.

I didn't read my first book until I was in my late 30s. So, I'm most definitely not the type to want to write one. But I have felt for many years a desire to bridge the gap between the scholastic literature for the well-educated and the "Parenting for Dummies." Maybe things aren't going so well in your family and you want them to be better. You came from a difficult upbringing and are scared that you won't be as good of a parent as you desire to be. Maybe things are going well, but you want to learn more. Maybe you want to be better prepared for the future and see your wonderful family reach their full potential. Whatever the reason is, I hope this book can be of assistance.

The first part of this book will help you get to know our humble beginnings a little better. It was rough. And I messed up a lot. I want to convey to you, reader, just how bad things were, because I never want you to lose hope or think your situation is "just too bad." Instead I want you to be excited for how good things can be! The second part of this story includes the lessons I learned along the way in being a husband and father my family could be proud of. And also, one that they could laugh at a lot.

Acknowledgments

I thank God for my parents who drove the value of faith, excellence and high standards deep within my being as a child. I'm thankful for every man and woman who breathed life into me as a youth. I'm thankful for every friend who has encouraged me and held me accountable. And I'm most thankful to God for giving me my wife and children, who have driven me to be a far greater man than I ever would have been without them. I hope that my writing inspires those who read it, knowing that every challenge and trial I've faced has been worth it. Every failure has been an opportunity for growth, and I count it the greatest honor in life to be called "Husband" by my incredible wife, "Father" by my two wild and wonderful daughters and "Pop-Pop" by my precious grandchildren.

I would also like to thank those individuals who assisted me in the editing of this project. To one of my best buddies Randall Collins: you are the man and I'm blessed to call you friend. Randall, you got the ball running and I'll be forever grateful. To Rick Steele, you have an amazing way of pulling things together and helping me see my writing from all angles. You are gifted and I'm so thankful for you. To Dana, I so admire you and thank you for your work on one of my favorite chapters. I'm proud to call you friend. To Doug, you are a gifted man who sees what something can be and then makes it happen. I admire you and thank you for your assistance on the book cover. To Chelsea and Callie, you were on the ground floor of this project and I'm so thankful for your input and your belief in me. To Emily, your insight and prayer has encouraged me so many times I've lost count. You are flipping wonderful. To Alyssa, you were my co-writer and I couldn't have finished the book without you. You took my words and my thoughts and fine-tuned them into more than I ever dreamed. You are amazing Big Gir. To Andi my beautiful wife, I live to love and serve you. You are my inspiration.

PART I
OUR STORY

Meeting Andi

I was divorced by the age of twenty-one. Is this a great way to start the story or what? The marriage was short, less than a year total, but the pain we both went through seemed to go on for quite some time. I do not blame the young lady I was married to. I blame myself for my lack of maturity. I didn't understand at the time that we were two very different people driving in two very different directions. I sure wish I had heeded the advice from my parents, my best friend, my pastor, and other close relationships that warned we weren't well-matched, or equally-yoked. I was angry, filled with regret, and had totally lost my sense of self-worth once everything was finalized.

I had completely given up on the idea of marriage in my future. I was adamant about this to everyone. I'll just wait tables, party, and go back to school later when I have the money. That was my plan: to selfishly make myself happy. I might have partied a lot, but inside I was miserable. I kept my emotions hidden. I faced the world with a smile and confidence, then went home to face my miserable reality and failure. It was a dark place in my apartment even when the lights were on.

I'd love to say that I learned from my mistake and "failed

forward" like I talk about later in the book. But I just wasn't that guy yet. For the next few months I chose to date heavily, and things just got worse. I made one mistake after another and I knew deep within that things would have to change. I was not the man I was raised to be. I have never been a man without purpose. If you had asked anyone prior to this, "Who is Jeff Harrell," they would have painted quite a different picture. They would have told you that I was respectful to those around me, a man who loved music and sang often in church, and a man who loves Jesus. These were the character traits deep within me prior to messing up. But this was not me at twenty-one. I just dated girls for the wrong reason in order to distract myself from who I really was. I pulled the blinders over my own eyes.

Being gifted as a sales person didn't help things at all. Since I was a young boy I had the ability to sell almost anything. I sold candy in school as a fourteen-year-old kid and actually made a lot of money. At one time I had hundreds of dollars stashed in my sock drawer. If it weren't for the threat of expulsion from my principal, I would have never stopped. It's a great gift to have if used for good. But selling a false impression of yourself only hurts those you love, including yourself. At this point in my life I didn't want marriage, and I didn't want kids, I just wanted my freedom. Why would anyone want anything else, right? Truly what I needed was a good butt-whooping and a change of heart.

Less than a year after the divorce, I met another girl through a mutual friend that waitressed at a nearby Shoney's. My friend wanted me to meet her around 6 am one morning. I woke up that morning, never brushed my teeth, had greasy hair down to my shoulders and wore a shirt that had been lying on the floor for I don't know how long. We finally got to Shoney's, sat down at a table, and one of the most attractive girls I'd ever seen rounded the corner and BAM! This girl wasn't just attractive. As she began to take our orders and asked how we were doing, I realized she actually had a personality and seemed so simple and easy to talk to. I sure wished I had arrived more presentable.

Within a few weeks, she started waitressing at the Ryan's restaurant where I was employed. I was clearly interested in her. But every waitress in the restaurant told her to stay far away from me and told her all the crazy tales of my past; they almost had her convinced that I wasn't worth the effort. I didn't even think that I was worth the effort. And I had practically painted across my forehead that I was only interested in a good time. But there was something about this new waitress that had me messed up physically and mentally. I finally made the move and at least tried to get to know her. There were no violins playing, no thoughts of riding in on a white horse; just one hundred percent hormones and a will to achieve.

So, after a lot, I mean a lot, of pursuing and flirting and cologne-bathing, I convinced her to go on a date with me. We finally went out, watched Tom Cruise fly his plane, and then, well, we messed up quickly. I know in today's world it seems pretty common to sleep with whomever you want to sleep with. But I grew up with higher standards. It wasn't ok then and its not ok today. All I knew was I couldn't stand to be away from her. This was different than I'd ever experienced before.

I wish I could tell you that we slowed things down. But we

definitely did not. In fact, we sped things up. My buddy and I were supposed to go on a trip to Mexico together, but he had to back out last minute, so I immediately put my sales cap back on and convinced her to come with me. I think at this time I had everyone around me confused. Where did the guy go that didn't want a wife or kids, but only wanted freedom? Well, he had left the building. Something about this simple gentle soul had me captivated. I had temporarily lost my mind. I was in love and wanted to be with her constantly. The plan to make that happen would develop quickly.

Well I guess you might be curious of what my parents thought at this point. I can tell you they thought I was crazy. But after meeting her they got on board quickly. When I told them there was a chance, a small chance, we might elope in Mexico, my dear mother hooked us up with info on how to get the blood test required for marriage in another country. She also gave us a contact at a jewelry store that could help us with some cost-effective (ahem, cheap) wedding bands. She was amazing.

Off we flew to Mexico for the time of our life, after knowing each other for only five to six weeks. I don't know if we could've been any more in love at this point. We both just knew that we wanted to be together. The place was breathtaking; the music was playing, and the smells on the street from the food vendors was incredible. We unloaded, hit the streets, and the adventure began. It was a little later in the evening the first night of our trip when smells from a hotdog stand got my attention. Maybe I was on the edge of starvation or maybe it was the aroma that got me, but I had to have that hot dog. My beautiful Andi softly warned me that maybe that wasn't a good idea. But I ate it anyway. It was mind-blowing good, and the flavor and memory of it still lives with me today, because for the next four days of our vacation I lived in front of my toilet and slept in the tub. When I throw up, I make sounds that border insanity. If our neighbor in the room next to us had not felt pity on me and given me the smallest white pill I'd ever seen, I would've surely died. I am not joking; I felt like death. Not the best way to impress a girl, but she didn't leave me. I knew then she must be a keeper.

We hadn't talked much about marriage. We just casually looked at the hotel pamphlet on weddings, set it up, and had a Spanish-speaking man marry us overlooking the pool at our hotel. It was beautiful—magical. And even though we never understood a word the preacher said, we meant our vows and were determined to make our marriage work. We walked back to the room; I excused myself so I could throw up again, and then we met some new friends for dinner. My new wife and I experienced two different "honeymoons." She became tanned, cultured, and well-fed. I became whiter, ten pounds lighter, and cynical toward street vendors. I'll never forget it, and neither will she. We came back from that trip happy and committed to each other and with stories for a lifetime. This woman, of course, is the wife I have been married to for over thirty years and is the mother of our two daughters. Thank God for his mercies, his forgiveness, and his love for us.

We returned home from our trip, and then reality set in. We had very little money, had to move in with my parents, and soon realized we knew next to nothing about each other. This was not a fairy tale story, not even close. The truth is, we were so much in love we didn't even notice the incredibly difficult circumstances that we were in the midst of. We soon moved out of my parent's house so we could start our own memories in our own place and not sleep in a bedroom right off of my parent's living room. That was rather awkward to say the least. We loved our first apartment. We loved coming home each night and counting our tips to see if we could pay the bills that month. But it didn't bother us. We were crazy about each other.

Those first few months were tough; I mean, they were really tough. We moved from city to city as I moved into management with Ryan's Steakhouse. I was working seventy plus hours a week, sometimes doing six twelve-hour shifts in a row. As a young newlywed making really good money and with no college degree, I felt that I was doing pretty well for myself. God gave me the innate ability to communicate, problem-solve, and lead others in very challenging circumstances, and the restaurant world gave me great opportunity to hone those skills. Andi's belief in me was a huge part of my success. With as many hours as I was working, Andi to this day isn't sure how she got pregnant with our firstborn, Alyssa. I basically saw my wife one day a week and typically used that time to sleep. But three years into our marriage, it was time to start a family, and the long hours and restaurant culture was not ideal for raising a family. In a short period of time with the company, I could name three broken marriages, three managers that routinely cheated on their wives, and another manager that was in his fourth marriage. Most of the management were sucked into a world that revolved around how much money they could make or how hot the next waitress was they just hired. And Andi was starting to forget what I looked like. We both knew things had to change and change quickly.

After researching a lot of different options, an opportunity opened for me to become a buyer for the Belk department store chain in Atlanta. It would provide more stable hours and a healthier work environment, so I started my training in Chattanooga in hopes to move up quickly within the company. At one of the last training sessions, which was actually in Atlanta, a nicely dressed man stopped me and asked me if I was "here for the interview." Well, I had no idea what he was talking about, but he led me into his office to "interview" me for what I assumed was a final step in the process of me becoming a buyer. However, it was actually an interview to become a Personnel Operations Manager for the store. I looked at him stunned and quickly apologized. "Oh, sir I'm here in the buyer's training program. I didn't realize this was for a management position." That man sat back in his chair and shrugged, "Well, I like ya. You want the job?" And just like that I was in a management position again, this time in the big city of Atlanta. I don't know all the details of how God works. But it seems to me that he was always aware of who he wanted me to be and orchestrated all the changes necessary to get me there. We weren't big into faith or church at that time. But we were always thankful and aware of every blessing. My salary was substantially less for a while, but in (Romans 8:28-29, NKJV), Paul told the Romans, "And we know that all things work together for good to those who love God, to those who are called according to His purpose." Now back to Andi being pregnant…

Our First-Born Cone Head

I so vividly remember being in the emergency room. It seemed like the whole world had accompanied us to the hospital. The room smelled like fast food and everyone had opinions on what the baby would be like, what we should name her, and what we should do once she was born. I could hardly process it all. My system was on overload, and I was shutting down mentally.

I remember being blown away with the entire process. Rolling Andi into the labor and delivery room, the ice chips, the weird breathing, and of course the scar on my hand that still bares proof of the moment before they gave her the epidural. Then, it was go time. Andi pushed, pushed, repositioned, yelled, and cried. She managed to still look like an angel, despite her hospital gown and horrendous breath. (We had been there for… an eternity.) After quite some time, it was clear that she had exhausted her energy, and the baby didn't want to budge. I remember when the doctor uttered the words "C-Section" in the event that Andi was too exhausted to push anymore. I wasn't even sure what that meant, but I knew the operation would involve cutting open my wife. I looked over at her in a moment of hysteria and said, "Push Andi!! They're going to cut you open!" I may have also used expletives to get my point across. It proved effective as Andi pushed hard, and our little baby girl practically flew out.

My oldest daughter is now a beautiful woman. When she came out of the womb, that might have not been my first thought. Her head looked like the orange caution cones you see during road work. "Oh my Lord, we gave birth to a cone head," I thought. I remember afterwards telling Andi, "Baby, you've done it! I'm so proud of you!" I looked at the doctor and asked, not so discreetly, "Will her head stay that way?" He looked at me like he wanted to hurt me and said a flat, "No, it won't." I didn't ask him anymore questions.

Something happened inside me when that little girl was placed in my arms. I lost it. Every bit of nervous humor and tough exterior just melted away. I was a dad, and life would never be the same. I knew this would forever change our lives. The next few days and weeks were a blur, as Andi and I tried to work through sleep deprivation. Alyssa came out singing and hasn't stopped since.

We were in a small apartment then, and I sure didn't grasp my role as a dad. I understood the providing aspect but couldn't change a diaper to save my life. Not only did we have adjustments as new parents, but we had obstacles to overcome as a married couple as well. We really didn't have any friends our age that had small children. To make things worse, we didn't know the proper way to communicate our feelings to each other. I was very impatient in those days, something I still have to work on today.

I thought we were absolutely going to lose our sanity in that tiny apartment. But as we all know parenting does get easier.

I remember having a full day off from work, and Andi left me to experience what it was like to be a parent. My child screamed for over ninety-percent of the day. She turned shades of purple I had never seen. At one time, I placed Alyssa in her crib where she'd be safe and walked out to the balcony. I looked up to the sky and prayed for help. But I couldn't even hear myself! Her screams were coming through the walls as though they were thin as paper. Isn't it wonderful though that just when you think you can't take anymore, God gives you the strength to breathe and compose yourself? I had a moment of clarity out there on that tiny porch. My child was so unresponsive to me because she spent most of her time in the arms of her mother. She barely ever heard my voice except early in the morning and sometimes at night. I never got up at night; only on rare occasions did I help do anything. Andi was miserable away from family in Atlanta, and since she was the one raising Alyssa, we decided it would be best to move back to Chattanooga closer to our friends and family. Our family and faith were the glue that held everything together.

A New Job and an Old Car

As months went by, it seemed to get easier. Alyssa started mouthing weird words that made me laugh, would get up in her crib and rattle it as though she was a rabid animal and started showing a cool little personality. I wanted to be a more present dad but still saw provision for the family as my main goal. I took a job with Circuit City as a salesperson in hopes of making more money. I had dreamed of working at Circuit City since I was a young man, but they had always required a degree or so many years of experience. You'll find out later that I only had an associate degree—only because my mother pulled some strings at a local community college that doesn't exist anymore. I'm still not sure how I got the job other than God. At this point, we were in a little cottage in Red Bank, TN. It was an older home, and we were so excited to be back in our hometown. I was bad at a lot of stuff, but spending money was my greatest problem. I could make it; I just couldn't manage it very well. I knew when I started at Circuit City there was a great opportunity to make a lot of money after I got my feet wet and learned the ropes. It was a six- to eight-week process to train, and we were quickly short on money and in our first financial crunch. To say we were scared was an understatement. We had one car, a couple cans of beans, a loaf of bread and bills to pay. I started working as many hours as I could to try and get us out of the financial mess we were in.

On a cool crisp morning with the sun shining and the birds chirping, reality finally found me. And it wasn't very kind. I walked out of the house to breathe in the smells of fall, and to my surprise I found my neighbors were all outside as well. Only they weren't enjoying the weather. They were staring at my car as it got repossessed and towed out of our driveway. Oh, what a beautiful morning!

After watching the tow truck drive off, our friendly neighbor offered to sell us his old car in the back yard in the knee-high grass. You'd think this was a nice gesture, and I think he really wanted to help us out. But that was the sorriest car I had ever seen. I followed him to his back yard and lifted up a dusty tarp to find a 1970 Renault. After getting stung by a few wasps hiding under the tarp, I jiggled the keys into the ignition and wondered how I ended up here: in this dusty old car that was supposed to take me to work in the morning, assuming the bungee cords would hold the back two doors from flying open. I worked all day on it, washing it, waxing it, and used up an entire can of W-D 40. Seriously, I don't know if it was more embarrassing to have my neighbors watch my car get repossessed or pulling up to work every day in that Renault.

Eventually I found the strength to walk back inside of our home and tell Andi what was happening. We laugh about it now, but the scene on the inside of our home that day was anything but laughable. Andi was rocking in a chair in the living room holding on tightly to Alyssa. There was worry and anxiety in her eyes. I wanted to hold both of them and make it all better. I was just too embarrassed and challenged with who I was. I was a devastated man. I thought maybe if I let Andi be alone for a little while and played with Alyssa I would feel better. I reached for Alyssa to come to me and she turned her head into her mom's side. I did it again and this time Alyssa yelled, "No!" I asked Andi to tell her to come to me but that did not work and made the moment even tenser.

Something inside of me broke. All this time I had used the excuse of being "provider" as the reason I couldn't help out with Alyssa. Now I wasn't even the provider. I didn't know who I was. It still hurts today as I think about it. My eyes are glassy as I write these memories. They are still as clear to me today as they were then.

I went for a drive in my dreadful car and stopped somewhere on the side of the road and lost it. I cried until I couldn't see straight. All I could see when my eyes opened was the disappointment on my wife's face, the tiredness in her eyes, and the face of my child that I barely knew. I decided on that day, in that terrible car, that something had to change. And I begged God to help me know what it was I was supposed to do. I was not going to lose my family.

I didn't make a ton of progress overnight, but from that day forth I sought out wisdom. I talked with people who had healthy families and asked them every question I could think of. Many of those families are still our friends today. I'm thankful for a church who believes in family and reminded us that no one is responsible for raising our kids but us. I made a commitment to my family to do the following three things:

1) Have a relationship with Jesus Christ. (I couldn't do any of this as successfully as I wanted to without his guidance.)

2) Never let a career take precedent over family.

3) Serve my wife instead of seeking to be served. My wife comes before anything. If she was going to be my wife for life, then my relationship with her was key to the future of our family.

If we as men and fathers could wake up every day with one thought on our minds, "How can I best serve my family today," the world would be a different place. As things at home began to get better and Andi and I sought to apply these healthy principles to our life, things at work began to improve as well. I became a top agent for the company and was one of the few employees without a four-year degree. Finally, we were in a good place, mentally, spiritually, and financially.

It was the three of us taking on the world. Alyssa was two years old and had practically taken over my work place. Everyone at work knew that my family was the source of my joy. And it was that joy that got us through all the crazy transitions we've experienced in life. It was during this season of life that I learned the value of laughter. You can get upset at your daughter when her leaky diaper seeps onto your new suit, or you can laugh. It's really that simple.

And Then There Were Four

While going one hundred miles per hour on the sales floor at Circuit City, I caught a glimpse of my wife standing off in the distance with a very strange look on her face. It was normal for my wife and my daughter to visit me on the sales floor, as this might be the only time they see me till late in the evening. I was in the middle of a huge sale, and it took me longer than usual to get to her. As I approached her, I could tell she had something important on her mind. This might be the only time I remember anyone looking confused, bewildered, and joyful at the same time. Yep, she dropped the bomb that the stork would soon be visiting our house again. I can't remember my exact reaction but I'm sure it wasn't the right one.

Alyssa, our first daughter had nuclear energy, only needed two hours of sleep a day to survive, and was the craziest wonderful thing we'd ever experienced. She was three kids wrapped up in one body, so my initial internal response to the new baby coming was, "Oh my can we really handle another one?"

Long story short, the answer was YES. Of course, we can.

Change is difficult, but it can be so inspiring. Her second pregnancy was perfect, and after she was born, we, I mean I, was relieved to find that she didn't have a cone head like our first one. God knew us so well, and He knew we needed two girls. Both girls were so very different, one singing non-stop and the other cuddled up on the couch 24/7 but both fit perfectly into our future.

The Pink House

The four of us lived in a tiny pink house by the time Emily came along. Yes, it was pink. And it was a mere 760 square feet. This time around I wanted to play more, not work more. I loved being a dad. And I might have not said it at the time, but I loved our crazy little pink house. It was in that cramped space that we learned about each other. We learned how to have faith in God. To trust him with what little we had and forgive ourselves, or myself, when I nearly burned our house to the ground.

Yep, I almost burned down that little Barbie pink house. There was a blizzard in 1993. The only one we'd had in years, and although the weathermen forecasted snow in mid-March, no one believed them. So, when the power went out and the snow came down in thick heavy blankets, we were quite unprepared. We put all the food from our refrigerator into the snow to keep it cold and decided to make the most of it. Alyssa built multiple snowmen, and our newborn Emily was cute all bundled up in blankets. What a picturesque scene! I decided I would make use of the wood stove in the middle of our house. I had just bought a new saw and had tons of landscape timbers in my yard to use for firewood. Well, as most humans know, this was a bad idea. A really bad idea. I cut the wood into perfect sizes, found a box of matches and started a glorious fire. There were a couple of things I hadn't quite thought about. I didn't know how to use a damper, the lever that controls the fire, and I didn't know landscape timbers were soaked in a chemical that was deadly to inhale. Andi's favorite show was *Little House on the Prairie,* and I had envisioned us all snuggled up to the sounds of the wood crackling while we warmed our hands. Within minutes the house, the entire house, was about 80 degrees and filled with green smoke. I don't remember that from any of the *Little House* episodes. We opened all the windows and doors and froze until the green billows of smoke were gone. After we knew we were going to live, we just celebrated for a few days; wore four layers of pajamas to bed and built snowmen until we couldn't feel our fingers anymore.

Those days in that little cottage laid the groundwork for our future. We didn't have everything we would have liked at the front end of our start as a family, but that never held us back. Andi and I grew closer than we'd ever been. Emily and Alyssa became inseparable and practically still are today. Being a husband and dad became a daily top priority. Emily and Alyssa were so different. Alyssa had to share every thought in her mind, and Emily would sometimes go hours without saying a word. We appreciated their differences and watched them bond and grow together. I believe when they were young they knew they were our priority. They were loved unconditionally and equally—with our never showing favoritism in any way.

You don't need a nice fancy house to be happy. By the time we had Emily, we had already moved half a dozen times. And the car you drive around in may be a bit embarrassing, but life is about the ones that are in the car with you. Your marriage may not seem like the perfect fairy tale others have, but give it to God, be smart about the friendships you have in your life, and honestly, God can make something out of absolutely nothing.

PART II

LESSONS LEARNED

Now that I've told the story of how our little family began, I want to share with you the more specific life lessons I learned while trying to balance family and business. It is important to me that you know my beginnings were rocky and not ideal. Because I believe every person has the potential to raise a healthy family and be successful in business as well. I have provided questions at the end of each chapter to allow you time for self-reflection.

Life Lesson No. 1

A New Branch on an Old Tree

We live in a world full of dysfunctional families. We all know heart-breaking stories of children who lost their way because of selfish parents or broken homes. Unquestionably, external factors—the death of a parent at an early age, financial difficulty, or some other tragic circumstances, can make parenting difficult or even impossible. Thankfully, I don't know what those specific hardships feel like, nor do I want to experience any of them in my home. None of us, however, are immune to adversity. We all must deal with difficulties of varying degrees; however, some must deal with crises of a more devastating nature. My heart goes out to those who struggle to rebuild their lives after a significant loss.

That being said, people survive and triumph over unspeakable tragedies every day, and their victories give all of us hope. I admire and respect single parents and grandparents who have overcome tragedy and continue to give their children and grandchildren amazing love and support. What inner strength and incredible faith those individuals must have! I am so thankful for them.

I've titled this chapter, "A New Branch on an Old Tree." When I speak of being the "new branch on an old tree," I am not necessarily talking about people who have overcome tragic situations. I'm referring to children and young adults who have paid a steep price because of their parents' failures. I'm talking about the innocent victims of substance abuse, immorality, physical abuse, destructive lifestyle changes, desertion, laziness, and countless other selfish and harmful abuses inflicted on them by those who were supposed to protect and nurture them. These children and young adults have been hit hard. As a result of their parents' behavior, they suffer mentally, emotionally, socially, and physically.

But I choose to believe there is still hope for dysfunctional parents and the children affected by their actions. In fact, I'm investing the second half of my life on it. I have written this book for this very reason: to see change in the hearts of as many families as possible.

Nothing pierces my heart more than hearing a young married couple say, "Why would we bring a child into this messed-up world?" Most of those who make this statement are the victims of dysfunctional, selfish parents. They can only perceive a world like the one they grew up in. I have heard this statement from so many young adults. I am sickened to see what their painful upbringing or the state of our world has caused them to believe.

The truth is, you can never cut down the family tree into which you were born, *but you can grow a new branch on that tree!* Every person getting married today, regardless of their age, has the power to start a new branch on the family tree and build a new legacy for their family.

If you and your spouse desire to have children, please do it. Get busy conceiving them or adopting them. If your childhood was far from idyllic, rise up out of the ashes of dysfunction. Take your broken past and use it to build a new future, both for you and your descendants.

You are *not* caught in a vicious, inescapable cycle of dysfunction and failure.

You are *not* destined to follow in your parents' destructive footsteps.

Show the world what you've got! You know the right way to live, and, if you don't, be smart enough to seek wisdom.

You—the new branches—are the hope of my generation. There are many in my generation who want to see you succeed, and we are willing to help you. If you need mentoring, seek it. We all need the support of meaningful relationships. If you have no parents to lean on, seek an experienced parent out you know you can trust. Let those who are willing dive in and help you.

Your mentors are here for you. We are in your churches, your workplaces, and your neighborhoods. Some of us are in your schools. Others of us are involved in community programs started and funded by people who care about you, even if they do not know you. Seek us out; we are here to help you.

I am grateful to have had a number of mentors in my life, and I still have meaningful relationships with many of them today. Mentors are invaluable and necessary as we grow through life.

Don't sit back and wait for them to come to you. Surround yourself with people you respect. Soak up their wisdom. Someday, you will have the opportunity to bless someone else with what they taught you, maybe even your own children.

Do not let this messed-up world rob you of what God intended you to be. He has a good plan for your life, a future and a hope (Jeremiah 29:11, NKJV). Be a new branch on an old tree: Build your own legacy.

I'm so adamant about this because I've seen first-hand that it can be done. Here are the ways Andi and I implemented this "be a new branch" idea into our family.

As I write this chapter, I want to make sure you know that I experienced a first-class upbringing and was, for the most part, the envy of my friends. When I speak of things that Andi and I chose to change or tweak on our old tree, I'm speaking of changes that fit our personalities better and the vision we had for our future. Our new branch had to fit us and not anyone else. Our new branch is our new legacy, and the changes we made, though sometimes difficult, only strengthened our new branches. So how did we start growing our new branch? How did we start tweaking the changes we felt necessary?

First, Andi and I had to recognize all the great things our parents did and find value in our upbringing. For now, I will use my personal childhood experience to illustrate this concept. I understood even at an early age that my world was far better than that of most of the kids with whom I grew up. I was surrounded by a lot of broken marriages, and my friends were very willing to share what life at home was like for them. When I went home to both of my parents and the security and peace of their healthy marriage, I knew I had it extremely good. There were several things we did as a family when I was growing up that I wanted to make sure I did with my family:

1. **<u>Family Night</u>** - Every Thursday night we all sat in our living room and watched the *Waltons* and ate Ruffles® chips and French onion dip. At the time I acted like it annoyed me. But deep down, I really loved it. It was peaceful and relaxing. We talked about our week, and no family member could skip out. It was strictly family time—no golf, no dishes, no distractions. In our household, we took family night to a whole other level. In fact, there were few nights that weren't family nights. We all ate dinner at the table together when we were home, and most nights ended with us around a board game or watching a movie together.

2. **<u>Excellence</u>** - My dad was unusually obsessed with his tools, his garden, and his yard. He would spot a leaf on a freshly cut lawn a hundred yards out and immediately go pick it up. My dad worked tirelessly to make sure his garden grew properly. He took pride in his yard. He taught me that hard work produces something pretty spectacular, and that nothing happens instantly. As a teenager, I hated mowing and weed eating. If it wasn't singing or girls I wasn't interested.

   Once I started buying my own tools and had my own home, I understood better. Today I don't garden, but I now love what comes out of it. My dad is seventy-five and still has a killer garden. I'm sure my dad often thought that what he was telling me about soil, fertilizer, seasons, rainfall, and gardening fell on deaf ears. But it didn't. Just because a child seems uninterested doesn't mean he or she is not listening. I learned some crucial life lessons during this time—lessons that have blessed me tremendously as an adult. I've successfully finished remodeling a house (with a lot of help from friends) with tools that I wouldn't have even known how to use as a teenager. And my lawn and landscaping are immaculate. You see, there are things you take with you, even if you don't realize it when you're young. With his tools and his garden and his lawn, my dad taught me to value that which contributes to my success, to work with excellence, diligence, and perseverance, and to take pride in my work and possessions. I passed these lessons onto my children, and they have benefited greatly from understanding that you must work hard consistently and persevere to produce positive results.

3. **<u>Communication</u>** - My dad was also a great storyteller, and he loved to make people laugh. I can't repeat some of his stories because I shouldn't have been listening through the air conditioning vent! Just picture the scene from the movie, *A Christmas* Story, where the dad fights with the furnace. He was a spectacular salesman and communicated with other adults with a master's touch. He could sell anything and often did. I chose to take with me into my own family and career my father's talent to communicate effectively with people and make them smile.

4. **<u>Seeing the greater good in others</u>** - My mother was caring, selfless, and convinced I could do no wrong. She always wanted my sister and me to have more than they could really afford. She worked hard, really hard, all her life until the early stages of Alzheimer's set in. She only spoke positive things about people and hated when someone degraded another person. She loved and encouraged us with every breath she took. Mom had an incredibly difficult childhood in a broken family and spent much of her younger years in an orphanage. She never blamed her past or let it crush her future. In an interesting turn of events, the orphanage she lived in actually funded a portion of my children's college education. It was so inspiring to me to know that children who grew up in a less-than-perfect world would want to later bless others by pouring time and finances into the education of the next generation of children. Only children of parents who attended the orphanage received this blessing. Pretty cool, huh? God took the bad and made good from it. I gleaned from my mother her gift of tenacity and her desire to stay humble and kind to others.

5. **<u>Fighting for what matters</u>** – Mom wasn't able to go to college after high school, but she was determined to further her education. As a forty-five-year-old, she went to a community college and got her associates degree. She made straight A's while supporting her family and working a full-time job in collections. She didn't like excuses, especially mine. Mom lost the battle against her disease on September 22, 2015, but I believe she held on and fought harder than

most because she was not the type to give up. She was a fighter, and so is my father. They had been married fifty years when she passed away. My wife and I chose to make sure that no matter our circumstances, we would fight hard for our marriage. And we would believe in and fight for our children.

Even though I most often want to ponder on the positives, there were things I wanted to change or maybe do a little different. These next few paragraphs aren't meant to challenge the integrity of my parents or belittle their sacrifices as parents. Every generation has a new perspective on parenting, careers, and marriage. I'd like to say the changes Andi and I made concerning our family were all conscious decisions, but they weren't. A lot of them just happened. The challenge comes when we know we should change something but don't because either we're afraid of change or we think the old way is the easiest way. This never benefits anyone. To challenge the past is how we grow. So here are some things that we "pruned" when starting our family:

1. A personal passion of mine is music. It is just second nature that we hope our children will share the same interests, right? If I were a pro-football player, it would give me great joy if my son joined me in my passion. It just makes sense. This would make it easy for me to encourage, train and support him. Unfortunately for my sports-loving family, they birthed a son who had very little interest in sports. To this day, I have never watched a sporting event

from start to finish. My parents loved to hear me sing and fully supported me but I'm not sure that they really ever understood just how much I didn't care for sports. A child who truly respects and honors his parents, desires to please them, right? So, I played some sports with minimal success but knew deep down inside that sports just weren't my thing. The truth is, when sports were played on TV so frequently in our home, it felt like exclusion not inclusion. When a parent and child have different interests, it can be a point of disconnect and frustration. I wanted to be more aware of this with my kids and make sure that they never felt disconnected because we didn't have the same passions or interest in hobbies.

2. My sister and I grew up with some pretty strict rules around the house. Of course, every child feels about ninety-five percent of them are extremely unfair. But even at an early age I knew they were necessary. Even though there were rules in place, my parents could've been stricter. Today's world demands more structure in a family than ever. It's a darker world than we grew up in. I'm sure sometimes our children must have thought the only word we knew was, "No." I'm not sure I'd disagree with them. Andi and I chose to set clearer boundaries for our kids, but we clearly communicated the reason we said it. We were always happy to tell them why we had particular rules in place. We weren't trying to be drill sergeants, but we had immovable borders in place that were not negotiable. Examples: we scrutinized their movie choices, made sure they were home

at decent hours, and always met and got to know their friends. This wasn't because we didn't trust them, but rather we wanted to help them make wise decisions that would keep them safe. We never used the world's standards in raising our own children.

3. I'm very aware that closed-door meetings and one-on-one private meetings are necessary in a marriage for various reasons, but I like open doors better, and so does my wife. We love to put it all on the table. I'm sure my parents never knew this, but closed-door discussions struck a little fear into me and my sister a few times when we were younger. Most kids at a young age have no idea whether they were the cause for the meeting or if it was something else that happened. Does this speak to you? Tension and stress within a home sometimes places more weight on a child's mind than the parent is ever aware of. My parents were very private people, and Andi and I are not. In fact, we are polar opposites. We chose to discuss the good and the bad in an open format no matter how great the challenge. This is how we faced these trials as a family. It works.

We must remember as seasoned parents, we are the only ones who will be held accountable for the raising of our children. It was never God's intention that the aunt, uncle, pastor, grandparents, or anyone else raise that child, even though circumstances may arise where family is called to step in. He said to the parents, raise the child up in the way he or she should go. Yes, sometimes people other than the parents have to raise kids for one reason or another, but we must acknowledge that the child is, first and foremost, the parents' responsibility.

You'll find that the "pruning" process isn't solely for family traditions. The environment and culture you are in may encourage ideas that as parents you don't agree with. Even though we raised our kids in church and had a great community of healthy people around us, we found that some things that worked for other families wouldn't suffice for ours. Here are a few things we did a little differently than what we saw around us.

1. First, we sought proven wisdom, not personal opinions. Unsolicited advice became unimportant, and I believe we actually told some individuals that as much as we appreciated their concern for us and our children, we would ask the questions and seek wisdom only from individuals who had proven results or had been through the fire. This was huge for us, and it offended some people, but I believe many people respected us because of it. We did not mean to offend. We as parents take in tons of data every day into our brain; it's up to us to separate the two or three nuggets of wisdom from the overwhelming flow of opinions. God will protect us if we ask him to guide us. That's a fact.

2. The second thing we changed was the world view of having our children involved in everything—making life so cram-packed that extracurricular activities became priority. I'm not questioning the value of sports, clubs, dance classes, and so forth. I'm questioning the fact that more often than not it becomes the focus, the priority and the meaning of life

for some kids and their parents. What we as parents place as high priority in our children's lives sticks with them. Sometimes sports work, and sometimes they don't. I've seen kids that just aren't ready for that kind of pressure and overwhelming expectations. We didn't want our children to feel that any event or activity they were involved in was their identity, that should they fail at the activity, they were failing us or who they were as a person.

I do see the value in extracurricular activities; don't misunderstand me. For some kids, a coach may be the closest thing to a father. Sports teach teamwork, integrity, character, and a commitment to excellence. So yes, there is value, but sports will never be a substitute for parenting. They will never be more valuable than life skills and definitely never be more important than friends and family. Might I offer a few different suggestions on how sports could be merged with empowerment? Here are a few: let's say Brian is my kid, and he's awesome, I mean really awesome, and everyone tells him so. Instead of painting a picture of his future that he himself might not even want, here is what I might say: *Son, you're an incredible pitcher. I'm so very proud that you practice hard and play even harder. Your ability to stay focused and your desire to do everything with excellence will help mold you into an incredible man. You are gifted, and I know you're thankful for it. There are scholarships available in some colleges for talented athletes. Is this something you would like to work towards?* (This is the question that's not often asked.) *What are your other interests? Which one excites you the most? You know I love to see you play, and if baseball is your dream job, I'll do everything I can to help you accomplish it. If it's not baseball, I'm fine with that. Whatever your passion, I want to help you achieve it. Son, what do you think makes you so successful as a pitcher? What makes you work so hard? What have you learned by playing the sport? Name three things you'd like to accomplish in life, so I can help you get there. If you don't know yet, that's alright. Everything you do right now will prepare you for whatever "it" is.* Let kids be kids. I believe they only want to know if we are going to be there with them no matter what they choose. You get my point.

My girls will tell you that I live by this principle. I wanted them to try new things and be well rounded in life—and they are. Neither one did well in sports, even though they tried, but life didn't end. My wife and I helped them find their strengths and focused on those instead of molding them into something they weren't cut out to be. Many parents want their children to be who they wanted to be more than finding out who the child wants to be. We did not do this. We focused on empowering them, making sure their friendships were quality friendships. We missed the mark many times, but the end results are evident in our children. They are well-rounded, empowered, happily married, beautiful, and successful. They see faith and family as priorities not possibilities.

3. A third decision Andi and I made was that we wouldn't force higher education on our kids; we only painted its

value. They caught on. I will neither allow someone's experience in college nor an absence of a degree to decide how I paint a full picture of that person. I find very little value in a college degree alone, but I do find great value in education and common sense. I believe we can be educated and trained in a lot of different ways, and not everyone is cut out or becomes successful because they graduated from college. In fact, it is a tremendous stumbling block to some who rack up huge debt and suffer because of it. Today's world is a little tricky as we place such importance on getting that document that states we finished four or more years of school. Of course, there are some professions that require a degree like a doctor or lawyer. I also don't want to diminish the value it has on one's psyche, but most schools don't prepare someone for the real world. Education without preparation is futile. Both of my girls graduated from very good schools and with very good grades. I'm so very proud of them and have told them so, but they know that attending college alone did not produce greatness in them, *rather their ability to present themselves with confidence and communicate their values would forge their career success.* If we could merge college, preparedness and money management into a curriculum, I'd sell it hard. But getting a degree simply because it's expected of them isn't the solution for all kids. My oldest needed a gap year to gain some perspective and get experience working before college. Let's stop teaching that no college equals no drive. It's simply not true.

So, to wrap it up, we chose then and will continue to choose what works best for us. We follow closely the instincts God gave us and move past our mistakes quickly, never stopping to dwell on the past. Legacy is what we leave behind; we move forward one generation at a time. Your new branch on that family tree can grow as strong and as full as you desire it to be. Ask God to help you and He will. He created it in the first place.

Life Lesson No. 2

You Can't Lead on "E."

At times in our lives, we all do it. We work too much, sleep too little, eat unhealthily, skip vacations, and let the wrong people suck the life out of us. We strive to be all things to all people while failing to see that we are wearing ourselves down in the process. To our own detriment, we are running out of gas and ignoring the warning signs.

It seems that leaders of businesses and organizations are most prone to this type of self-destructive behavior. I have found that most leaders are genuine servants. They are driven by a sincere desire to make a difference in the lives of the people and organizations they serve. However, their greatest strengths can also be their greatest weaknesses: their inherent need to satisfy others sometimes results in their failure to prioritize their own physical and mental well-being. Without realizing it, they are slowly destroying themselves. I failed to recognize that this was happening to me. Thankfully, something happened that forever changed my life—before it was too late.

At the age of 46, I had reached the pinnacle of my career. I was the operating partner for four Keller Williams Realty franchises that had not only survived but thrived through one of the worst housing markets ever. I was making more money than I had ever dreamed. Everywhere I turned, I was experiencing God's favor.

More importantly, I had a loving, supportive wife and two precious teenage daughters who honored and respected me. They were and still are everything to me, and I was grateful for all that God enabled me to provide for them. We had been on three vacations in the last six months, and my wife and I had just bought a cabin in the mountains—the fulfillment of a life-long dream.

Does this all sound good, or what? I should have been screaming "Hallelujah!" from the rooftops, right? From the outside looking in, my life seemed as close to perfect as it could be.

But on a chilly winter's day, I unexpectedly found myself in a crisis. On that morning, I drove to my office to give the speech of a lifetime to my employees and co-workers. All eyes would be on me as I enthusiastically presented my vision for the coming year. I take preparation very seriously. I had spent three full days preparing for this 45-minute speech. My partners in business depended on me to lead them, support them, and provide them a sense of security and accomplishment. And, on this particular day, I did not let them down. They gave my speech rave reviews. My presentation was seamless, and I could sense the entire room embracing my vision. As I walked out of the building and to my car, I savored how good it felt to have that presentation behind me. I was excited to go home and spend the weekend relaxing.

I had only been driving about five minutes when, unexplainably, my eyes started to water, and my face became flush with beads of sweat. What in the world was going on? Was I having a heart attack? A panic-attack? A breakdown? Should I call the doctor?

I am not exaggerating when I say that it was everything I could do to hold back my tears and compose myself. I was overwhelmed with something I had never before felt. I knew well what stress was, and this was far beyond stress: I was completely losing control. After three or four more minutes, I became so afraid of wrecking that I pulled over to the side of the highway. After shutting off the car, I cried out to God for understanding. I remember praying, *"I have it all, Lord. What is wrong with me?"*

I could not have prayed more earnestly, but no answer and no peace came. After a few more minutes, I restarted my car and drove directly home. For the next four hours, I sat in my office and stared out the window without moving. What was happening to me? Who could I call? If I called somebody, what would I say? This was the most confusing moment I'd ever experienced. As I sat there, I was finally able to compose myself. I called my wife just to check in. I faked a happy speech and made sure she knew I loved her. Then, I texted both of my girls a quick, "Your Pop loves ya!" Don't misunderstand: I was in no danger of hurting myself or anyone else. I just had an overwhelming feeling of loss and depression, and I didn't understand why.

Around 4:00 that afternoon my phone rang with the only call I remember from that day. I didn't want to answer, but it was one of my top agents who is also a personal friend. She was calling to see if I would join her on a talk show early the next morning. This was just not going to happen, so I politely told her I had something going on and would help her find someone else. I called everyone

I could think of, but with no success. Because of my great respect and admiration for her, however, I called her back and said I would join her.

That night was horrible. I couldn't let my family know how messed up I was, so I kept faking that I was okay. Later in the evening, I went back into work mode and pulled stats for the morning's discussion. I prepared for the next day like nothing had ever happened.

My dear friend picked me up early, and we chatted casually on the way to the radio station. The talk show went great, and on the ride home, I felt desperate to talk about what I was going through. But I didn't know how to explain it, so I kept my mouth shut.

As we neared my home, my friend handed me a book titled *Leading On Empty*, commenting that it was a good read and I should check it out. The author, Wayne Cordeiro, is the founding pastor of New Hope Christian Fellowship church in Honolulu, Hawaii. In the book, he tracks his battle with and recovery from burnout.

Did my friend know that this was exactly how I felt, like I was leading on empty? No one could have told her because I hadn't told anyone. How *could* I tell anyone about this and be sure they would keep it confidential?

I devoured the book, drenching its pages with a bucket of tears. *Leading on Empty* proved to be one of the most helpful books I have ever read. It pegged my condition while laying out a simple plan to help me get back on track. As I journeyed through its pages, I looked back over the last few years of my life and realized that God had shown me what seemed like a million warning signs that I was about to crash. At last, I recognized that I was out of gas. For years, I had been emptying my tank without ever thinking to refuel it.

Looking back, I may have been only days away from inadvertently making some really bad decisions. I tremble to think of the damage I may have done to my family, my partners, and myself had God not brought me to a breaking point. By prompting her to give me this life-changing book, the Lord had used my friend to rescue me without her even knowing it. I will be forever grateful to God and to her.

I share this story because there is no reason for anyone to get to this place, and if you are feeling empty, you can find your way back. I highly recommend *Leading on Empty* for anyone who desires to serve others. I also recommend it for everyone involved in leadership, both within the church and the corporate world.

Most importantly, I recommend Pastor Cordeiro's book and its principles as a father. You simply cannot have the energy to lead and love your family if you are drained mentally. Your family requires all of you.

Since reading *Leading on Empty,* I have embraced its principles religiously. Leading others and my family is my most passionate calling. Now, I am careful to refuel regularly and completely.

As a leader and parent, you must remember this: *it is impossible to fill someone else's tank if yours is empty.* Tragically, leaders make grave decisions when their tank is empty because they are too weary to recognize the severity of doing so. Even more tragic, they lose sight of the reality that they are risking what is right in front of them: their God-given gifts of family and future.

Here are a few of my refueling techniques. I share them in hopes that you will make your own list as well.

- I make friends a priority now. They are not an option. They are a huge source of encouragement, and some of them serve as accountability partners. Never underestimate the importance of surrounding yourself with people who fill you up, and don't drain you of your time and energy.

- When I vacation, it is all about refueling and no longer a time to strategize or consult on business matters. My wife and children deserve all of me. My family time is a source of energy that sustains me at work and keeps my integrity in check.

- I eat better, ride a bike, hike, and fly fish as often as possible. To say I don't have time to do those things really means I'm not organized enough nor focused enough to make rest and relaxation happen. This one mindset has rocked my world. If you don't have time for taking care of yourself either through exercise, diet, or recreation, make time.

- I still dream just as big as I ever did but I'm more strategic in setting realistic timelines to accomplish them.

- I read more, play more, and simply just enjoy the things that God supplies in nature that are free.

- Recently I decided that owning several companies wasn't for me at this time, and I practically transitioned my whole world to regain life balance. This gives me the time I need to plan for my next venture. Actually, writing this book will become a reality as a result of me reorganizing my life around faith, family, and life balance.

- I've chosen for a period of time to diligently work on personal growth and community impact instead of just financial gain. It is easy to write a check, but there's so much more power in putting our hands to the plow. I've made mission trips a priority, so I can help others who are hurting and remain humble and thankful for every blessing I've been given. I love the verse from (Luke 12:48, NKJV) "To whom much is given, much is required."

These are just some of the life balance techniques I use. They are simple and duplicable. Find what works for you and make them a priority, you owe it to yourself, your family and everyone around you, because your life holds great value.

The warning signs of burnout are different for every person, I'm sure. But I want to clue you in on some warning signs I personally experienced that I wish I would have paid more attention to. Maybe some of them sound familiar:

- **Loss of focus/short attention span.** A constant wandering mind for me should've been a clear warning sign. For the most part, I am acutely aware of my surroundings even when it looks like I'm not. So before I ran out of gas, I should have known something was very wrong. Even though I would prepare hours for a 30-minute meeting, it was harder to keep my concentration. Oddly enough, very few people caught it, and even odder than that, I had several people tell me they were inspired at the meeting or they noticed that I was focused. In reality, I had to think harder than ever. I felt drained after inspiring others, not empowered. This was a clear warning sign. I should have pulled some very close friends together and asked for a true diagnosis of my current self. I should have slowed down enough to find out why I was constantly drained mentally and physically.

- **Being short with those who actually care about you is a warning sign like no other.** For me, small problems seemed larger, I took casual remarks very personally, and sometimes my temper would flare without cause. My wife would ask, "How tall are you going to let the grass get?" The refreshed me would say, "I'm growing a crop of wheat for this winter." The burned-out version might say, "Maybe you'd like to try your hand at it." I found myself feeling short and sarcastic with those I loved. If you find yourself speaking and acting different than normal, it's a good time to analyze what's going on beneath the surface.

- **An overwhelming desire to withdraw from people and daily pressures is a sign of burnout.** I felt like an extroverted recluse. My life had revolved around being the focus of attention, the singer, the joke teller, the leader of the pack, and on and on and on, and suddenly I found myself wanting to be alone more than normal. I wasn't depressed, but I should have known this meant I needed to take charge of my time and energy. I should have learned when to say "no" and stopped spending time on those things or friendships that drained me.

- **Gaining weight quickly or losing weight quickly is another sign that something is not quite right.** I love to eat. So for me, frustration and a lack of drive equal weight gain. Before burn-out, I was at my heaviest weight in years. Even though I covered it well, it wasn't merely the extra weight itself. My pants were tight, which made me uncomfortable in meetings and travel. It made me more irritable. Looking at myself in the mirror made me more aware that this was not the "me" I wanted to be. My collars were tighter, I sweated more, and I wore more shirts at the beach and really didn't want to be in pictures. Psychologically we are more empowering and inspiring when we feel confident in our appearance. So, when appearances change, find out the reason. Don't just sluff it off and say it's just winter weight. Take charge and correct the problem ASAP. Have others keep you accountable. It's true that you look the way you feel.

- **Lack of intimacy.** We are most attractive to our spouses when we exude confidence and character. When we know who we are in Christ, and we're serving the needs of our family with excellence, we become very desirable to our spouses. I know this works. Sadly, the other side is true as well. When we are less desirable at home and our confidence levels are low, we become more attracted to those who are hurting, such as wives who aren't being treated well at home who want to feel loved at the workplace and vice versa. This is when the marriage comes under fire. So many men and women never see it coming until it's too late. Weariness and loss of self-worth altered their entire future. I've never been down this road, but I know countless men and women who have. If self-worth is low, so is self-morality in most cases. Know the God of all things brings us self-worth even at our lowest point.

To wrap up my experience with burnout and the lessons I've learned: no one knows me better than me. I know what makes me happy. I know when I feel tired, stressed, or unhealthy. Most importantly, anything that disconnects me from an abundant life will have to go. Love with everything you got—live a life in balance, and give God the thanks He deserves. Then you can be better prepared to be the parent and leader that will impact others around you.

Could you possibly be burnt out as well? Use these questions to evaluate where you are right now.

1. Do you see any warning signs in your own life that look like a burnout is coming? If so, write down the most vivid example, and share that challenge with someone you love and TRUST. It is crucial you work on one thing at a time. People who care about you depend on it, and you deserve a life that is in balance.

_____

_____

_____

_____

2. What changes do you need to make to maintain a healthy mind? Are there relationships in your life that need to be severed? Responsibilities that are burdening you instead of fulfilling you?

_____

_____

_____

_____

3. What do you do as a form of recreation? Who do you do it with, and when was the last time you did it? Recharging and refueling is imperative!

_____

_____

_____

_____

Life Lesson No. 3

Make Your Home "The Home"

Do you believe that it's important where your child spends his or her time? You bet it is! You can't and shouldn't control everything that your children do, but you should try to be a huge part of it. Work to build a home environment where no kid wants to leave. Yep, I said it: A home where no kid wants to leave. Provide a home that's safe, full of food (cheap food), clean (price of home doesn't matter), and welcoming to *all* kids, no matter their social standing or family structure. Having kids at our home for the past twenty-plus years has been the single most significant part of mine and Andi's lives. We've been given an incredible opportunity to mentor and to experience life at its fullest, all because we opened up our home to our kids' friends. In fact, if we had it to do all over again, we would've started hosting earlier and slept less.

Remember this: When you open your home, it may be the only real "home" another child may ever experience. Your home doesn't have to be perfect or void of arguments and drama. Remember, kids want it REAL. My wife and I started this process in an 800 square-foot home with very little food and a desire to impact lives. Even though our lives look much different now, the spirit in our home is still the same. What a joy it is to now see those same kids get married and achieve their life goals. There's no price you can put on that. These kids—now young adults—are family. I do want to make it very clear: Our home was just one of the homes that our kids and their friends chose to spend their time in. In fact, several of us parents alternated frequently. I can say this: every one of those families that opened their home to others is still healthy and strong today. That's pretty cool, huh?

How involved do you want to be? How important is it to experience your child's interaction with others? Take time to mentor, love, and care for children that aren't your own. You'll be blessed for it. Below I'd like to share a few snippets from some of the children that blessed us with their presence through the years. These were close friends of my children and still remain close today.

Emily Holden, friend of Alyssa's since 4th grade
I will never in my life forget staying up late with our girlfriends; playing games, chatting with our friends on the computer, and just loving each other's company. The environment in their home was so inviting and welcoming that it began to feel like a second home for me over the years. I always knew that when I went to Alyssa's house, I would leave feeling a little more inspired and a whole lot happier than when I arrived. Jeff and Andi were the type of parents to Alyssa and Emily that I hope to one day be to

my children—they welcomed their children's friends as if we were their own, and in the process, they taught me so much about what a loving, Christian home should look like. One thing that anyone who knows the Harrell family will tell you is that LAUGHTER is the backbone of their household. I remember one afternoon, Andi was driving us girls around in her super-cool, yellow Jeep Wrangler. It was a stick shift, and she showed me how to work the gears while she was driving. I had never felt cooler in my entire life! It's little memories like these that stick out in my mind about this amazing family. Jeff and Andi's healthy, loving marriage in a culture full of lies about divorce and separation was a beacon of hope for every one of Alyssa and Emily's friends throughout the years. The way that Jeff, still to this day, looks at his bride is nothing short of a Nicholas Sparks novel! I think the example they shared through their love for each other was the best thing they ever could do for all of the children that were in and out of their house throughout the years. I'd say the legacy they are leaving for their own family and for so many others that they have encountered throughout the years is nothing short of amazing!

Brynn Atchley, friend of Alyssa's since 6th grade
I feel like I lived at your house throughout middle school! Your family was like my second family. I always felt comfortable and never felt that I wasn't loved or wanted. All those sleepovers we had at your house! Five, six, or seven girls—all upstairs in your bedroom talking girl talk and making tons of noise. Never did they get mad or try to intrude. I always felt like your house was a safe place. Even back in the day when you had a sleepover with

ice cream sundaes and pajamas and I went home early because I got homesick. I love you and your family more than words can say. I can't think of a more open, loving, and hilarious group to be around. We were always surrounded with happiness and had the best influences I could have imagined!

Jacob Lepard, friend of Alyssa and Emily's since 9th grade
I became close friends with Jeff's daughters in early high school and have remained so into adulthood. His oldest daughter and her husband are some of my best friends, and his younger daughter married my college roommate. I spent many nights at the Harrell house with our group of friends over the years, playing games, watching movies, playing music, and just goofing off in general, as most high-schoolers (and fun-loving adults) tend to do. Throughout that time, Jeff and Andi did a remarkable job of being around and part of the fun, but yet still being parents. They clearly went out of their way to make their home an open and welcoming place to us, which eventually resulted in them feeling like a second mom and dad. As a teenage boy I always had the utmost respect for Alyssa and Emily, because I respected Jeff. He always took the time to be around and to know his daughter's friends, which was very impressive to me. Now that I have a family of my own, I look forward to making my home a similar environment and am thankful for the example shown by Jeff and Andi.

Megan Markum, friend of family since 7th grade
I've been visiting the Harrell home for over fifteen years. When you enter the house, you immediately feel at home because you

are family. They value spending time with people on the things that matter most. People are top-priority, and conversation is intentional and encouraging. We have laughed, cried, dreamed, and planned together because it was a safe space to do so. It is always a welcoming environment, and I look forward to every visit!

Amelia Hammon, friend of Emily's since elementary school
"Hey Em, want to come over?" "Not really. I'm watching *Friends* with my parents. Want to come over here instead?" That's usually how it went, which was fine with me. I liked going over to Emily's house. And not just because it was the first (and perhaps only) place I've ever had a fried bologna sandwich. Her dad is a hugger and always gave me a big one when I walked in the door. Her mom would take us for ice cream in the Jeep and French-braid my hair if I asked. I think what stood out most was how much they all *liked* each other. And you could tell in the little things. Her parents would be snuggled up together on the couch whenever we watched a movie. Her sister would come into the room and ask Emily and me about boys and actually listen. When we were upstairs dancing around in our pajamas in Emily's room, we'd hear her dad call out, "Whatcha doing Emily? I love you!" "I love you, Popsicle!" she'd call back. I always felt welcome, and I always felt loved! Like I got to join in on all the fun they were having together.

Jesse Morgan, friend of Alyssa's since high school and now husband of Emily!
I always went over to the Harrell home in order to seek guidance. I knew that it was a safe place to hash out my thoughts

and sort through tough circumstances life had thrown my way. I never felt judged as I expressed myself to understanding ears. And I always felt encouraged and empowered to persevere through whatever life may throw my way.

∞

Not only is it wonderful to hear and relive these comments from those special children who are now adults, but it's just as wonderful to know that my children were embraced in the homes of their friends as well. Even though there were moments of silence in our own home, my wife and I knew, without a doubt, that they were safe and loved in their friend's homes. It wasn't just the homes that made life different or special, it was being a part of a community that we trusted with our kids.

We made time for family, certainly. But sometimes turning family time into "friends and family" time was just the right answer. We didn't want our girls to be hermits, but we wanted to retain a strong family bond, even when they started pushing for more independence. So, we created an environment that was welcoming for all kids—a place where they could be themselves and feel safe. If I could have afforded to put in an indoor pool and playground when the kids were little, I would have done it. But instead, we had an $8 plastic pool from Walmart, dollar bags of tortilla chips and a sandbox full of ants.

Some questions to help you think about the kind of home you are creating:

1. Describe the feel of your home. Is it welcoming? Is it cold? Does it scream, "Get off of that!" or "make yourself comfortable."

   _____

   _____

   _____

   _____

2. If you have children, is your home "home base," or is it the last resort for your kids when they make plans with their friends?

   _____

   _____

   _____

   _____

3. If you'd like to improve on this, what would you change? How would you change it?

   _____

   _____

   _____

   _____

4. Our homes are where we entertain people we love, people we want to get to know, and people that we'd like to pour into. It's important that we make it a safe warm place. Write down some people that you'd like to entertain in your home. It could be some of your children's friends you

haven't met yet, a pastor, or a young person who needs some guidance.

_____

_____

_____

_____

The memories you make in your home help paint your future. Let me explain. The way your child feels loved determines what they'll look for in a spouse. The people that you laugh with and learn from in your home are the ones that will help you plan your child's wedding. The people that have helped guide you and spent time on your back porch praying with you are the ones instilling the strength in you to pour into others later on. Who do you want in that picture with you? Who do you want to be a part of your future? Maybe they're the ones who should get an invite to your house this week.

Life Lesson No. 4

What You Do Outside the Home

What happens when you're away from home will **always** impact you in your home. A wise man finds his self-worth in his faith and in the arms of his wife and family. A commitment to loving your spouse selflessly, sacrificially, and exclusively is the foundation of a phenomenal marriage.

Men, when you accepted the responsibility of being a husband, when you looked your bride in the eyes and said, "I'm committed to you till death parts us," you made a commitment to fidelity. You also committed to honor and respect her, to love her regardless of circumstances, and to serve her as the leader of the household. You guide the ship, provide its support, and serve the crew. This is what your commitment looks like.

Are you fulfilling your commitment faithfully?

You had better be. Your wife craves it, your children deserve it, and your home will not survive—much less thrive—without it.

On a broader scale, our nation's family structure is collapsing because so many men and women are neglecting and abandoning their responsibilities to their families.

I know personally how critical this commitment is. My first marriage ended in less than a year. Even though we did not have any children, it was still excruciatingly painful. While I was never unfaithful, I was definitely immature and selfish; I didn't really understand what serving my spouse actually meant. My immaturity led to wrong choices that not only affected me, but also my wife, as well as everyone else around me. As a result, I failed miserably as a husband in my first marriage.

Thankfully, after I messed up and almost gave up, I later grew up. I used those horrible mistakes to move my life forward. It didn't happen all at once. I'd be lying through my teeth if I said that once Andi and I got married I became a knight in shining armor. But we just kept learning and growing and making our commitment to each other a priority.

In June of 2018, my wife and I celebrated thirty wonderful years of marriage. We have been blessed with two daughters who are the light of our lives. In 2013, our older daughter, Alyssa, committed herself in marriage to a man whom I completely approved of and am thrilled to call my son-in-law. Emily, our younger daughter, followed suit in 2014, and I love her husband equally.

Our family talks openly about marriage. When we do, the conversation inevitably returns to the commitment to love, honor, and respect our spouses. Allow me to dig deeper into exactly what this vow means.

To me, the pledge to love, honor, and respect your spouse is the crucial factor that separates average marriages from exceptional marriages. In turn, this noble commitment leads to the growth of a family that can change the world.

I like to call this commitment the "Being Faithful Factor": if you love, honor and respect someone, you *will* be faithful to him or her.

Tragically, the definition of the word "faithful" in today's world has sorely diminished from what it used to be. In most people's eyes, the term is accompanied by a long list of *conditions*.

The world's view of faithfulness is something like this: "I will be faithful and love only my spouse as long as he/she lets me be myself (even if that changes), I have plenty of private time, the house stays clean, I'm allowed to pursue all of my hobbies, sex is geared towards my needs, and physical changes stay at a minimum If any of these factors change, I have the right to satisfy my needs as I see fit."

Doesn't this sound like the self-serving world we live in today? You bet it does. Because of this selfish attitude, marriages and families are being destroyed every day. Infidelity is becoming the rule rather than the exception. And we wonder why our country is in the shape it's in! Why have we closed our ears to this truth? Why does this not tie our stomach in knots? Is what we *want* more important than what our family *needs*? DO we care at all? The truth is: if we did, we would do something about it.

Selfish, uncommitted people need to be confronted with a blunt question: why get married and have children if you're not in it for the whole game? Why waste your time—and others' lives—at all? Marrying someone else when you have this attitude is the most selfish act of all.

As you can see, I'm very passionate about this subject. I believe that there is hope for every marriage when both spouses grasp what marriage and commitment really mean. Every decision you make matters, and none matters more than the decision to remain faithful to your spouse and children. I am faithful to my wife, first, because God gives me the strength to stay faithful, and, second, because I'm acutely aware of *how much it matters* to my wife, my children, and our community.

I'll tell you very simply what my commitment to wife looks like: in my opinion, I married "The Bomb" thirty years ago and she's still "The Bomb" today. Everyone in my world knows that this is how I feel about her. No one questions if I love my wife, because I don't give them a reason to period. My children, my family, and my friends know that her needs come before anyone else's on this earth. I have always strived to make my wife my number one priority. My girls knew their mom came first. Backing my wife in front of our children wasn't just important, it was imperative. I didn't always agree with her decisions, and neither did she with all of mine, but our children always saw a united front. There's a lot less dissension in the family when the children have parents who are united. God knows my heart for her, and He knows that, next to Him, she is my first priority. My children, friendships, and business all come after her.

Setting this priority early in a marriage is crucial to its success. I'm thankful that on every occasion this priority has slipped, my wife and I have realized it quickly. We immediately made the necessary changes to restore our relationship to first place in our lives.

So why all of this talk about commitment and faithfulness? Because as a 50-year-old entrepreneur and businessman, I have personally witnessed the unparalleled devastation that adultery unleashes on a family. I have painfully observed the breakup of scores of marriages, countless kids uprooted, and forever scarred, numerous businesses ruined, and great potential lost.

On another level, the death of a family—divorce—usually results in financial devastation for both spouses.

From my perspective, selfishness and infidelity are the two top causes of family devastation. We must do something to change this.

In my experience, the best way to combat unfaithfulness is through caution and accountability. Infidelity doesn't just happen overnight. We see caution lights flashing to warn us that our commitment to marriage is being tested. Instead of heeding them, we choose to ignore them and go on as we are. Or, even worse, we fool ourselves into believing that infidelity "could never happen to us."

As we disregard these warnings, we become increasingly numb to dangers that once alarmed us. Our innate defenses are no longer triggered by a lingering smile, an inappropriate comment, an awkward lunch, a flirtatious compliment, or an extended glance. Instead, we find ourselves indulging and enjoying these not-so-subtle signals from someone looking for self-worth outside of his or her marriage.

Wherever you are in life right now, *please* pause for a moment and recommit to being faithful to your spouse and your children.

Allow me to suggest some ways that you can safeguard your

marriage. Admittedly, some of these are unconventional, but I hope that they will speak to you. Both husbands and wives should adopt them and adhere to them sharply.

1. *Work hard to impress your spouse.*

   In the beginning of our relationships, we go to great lengths to impress our partners. We open car doors, dress our best, shower often, initiate romantic dinners, wear cologne or perfume, call each other pet names the list goes on and on. Remember the special things you did?

Remember how it made you feel to put forth your best in an effort to win the heart of this person? Remember how you felt when this person constantly put forth his or her best for you? As we become comfortable in our relationships with our spouses, we stop "wowing" them as we should. We become complacent toward making them feel special as well as toward making them feel that we are special. If we are not careful, we will stop trying to impress them at all.

I am committed to not letting this happen in my most vital relationships. *I* will be the one who impresses my wife. *I* will be the one who awes and inspires my children. It's *my* place to do this—not another man's. If you make yourself special for your spouse and children, they will have no reason to look elsewhere for excitement or inspiration.

2. *Flee Temptation; don't walk, run.*

   The wedding ring no longer means what it once did to many who see it on a person's finger. To some—hopefully the majority—it still means that the person wearing it is off the market. Others, however, view it as a daring challenge to be conquered. To them, the wedding ring makes the individual even more desirable. With that in mind, awkward conversations and situations will unquestionably present themselves in a married person's life. A few may arise innocently, but most will be initiated by someone with a clear agenda. Again, they *will* come, and we need to be prepared for them when they do.

The problem is, we don't always address the awkwardness quickly enough or boldly enough. Let's face it, who doesn't like to be told we look great or smell good or that we're awesome? We all love it. The truth is, being noticed and appreciated lifts our spirits and encourages us.

But when these comments come from someone other than your spouse, they are potentially deadly. You need to throw up every one of your defenses and not let them affect you too deeply. Furthermore, you need to respond instantly in a way that communicates that you are off limits.

You know when a comment or compliment is inappropriate, so treat it as such. If you don't make your standards known in the beginning, whether it's in the work place or at school or the grocery store or even at church, the opposite sex will continue to test your boundaries.

When I started dating, I loved a good strong "no," even though I got a lot of them! I appreciated a black and white answer instead of a flowery and vague response—one that insinuated a lack of interest, but left room for wonder.

Flowery words aren't real responses, they're invitations. For example: a man asks a woman if she'd like to grab coffee, knowing she is married. The woman responds by saying, "Aww, you are so sweet. I can't today, but thanks for asking!" She may mean to decline politely and graciously, but to the man, she is inviting him to ask again another day. She has failed to communicate that she does not want to have coffee with this man.

Or, say a woman is flirting continuously with a married man at work, coming into his office incessantly and touching his arm while she talks. The man always responds kindly and occasionally touches her as well. By responding this way, he is sending a clear message, even if he does not intend to. And he is inviting temptation to creep its nasty head into his life.

Indulging flirtatious behavior is like toying with a poisonous snake: if you don't cut its head off, it will bite you and kill you.

3. *Set boundaries.*

 Set firm boundaries for your interaction with the opposite sex. A relevant example: Never allow yourself to be in the car alone with a person of the opposite sex—not even for one block!

Sound a little extreme? Maybe so, but if the old saying, "perception is reality" stands true, why take the chance? Why test wisdom that's already been proven? Men, how would you feel if you saw your wife get into a car with another man? Wives, what would you think if you saw your husband riding with another woman? Or what will other people assume if they see you? They will jump to the same conclusions *you* jump to when you see someone you know driving with someone of the opposite sex other than his or her spouse: "Maybe she is test-driving a new car or maybe he is going to lunch with a coworker—but maybe not . . ."

Don't do anything that arouses suspicion and questions. Even more importantly, don't put yourself in a situation that might cause you to be tempted.

My wife and I have agreed to adhere strictly to this practice for years, and it works. In the last fifteen years, I violated this policy one time and learned my lesson. Had God not protected me, it could have proven fatal to me and to my family. A short time later, I found out that this woman whom I respected so highly was actually cheating on her husband. My naïve eyes were suddenly opened wide when I realized that, because I trusted *her*, I had let my guard down for the sake of convenience. What if people had suspected me as the other man in her life? What if their perception had become their reality?

For my wife and me, *there are no exceptions to this rule!* Our world loves a juicy, messy drama, but I refuse to be a leading character in one.

Along these same lines, be extremely careful with business lunches. Always meet for lunch in public, and, if at all possible, use the "three or no me" rule.

In our lifetimes, we have seen multitudes of scandals involving religious ministries and leaders. One preacher whose faithfulness to his wife has never been questioned is the world-renowned evangelist Billy Graham. Neither he nor his closest associates ever faced a single accusation of sexual impropriety. Why? Here's the answer in Graham's own words:

> "We pledged among ourselves to avoid any situation that would have even the appearance of compromise or suspicion. From [the day we made that pledge], I did not travel, meet, or eat alone with a woman other than my wife."[1]

People will respect the boundaries you set, and they will judge you by them. You have a gut instinct and common sense—use them.

4. *Be especially cautious when traveling alone.*

    Traveling alone is a necessary part of many people's careers and lives. Unfortunately, it can present distinct temptations. To protect myself and my family, I strictly adhere to the following "to do list" when traveling, and I strongly recommend that you do the same:

    • Wear your wedding ring proudly at all times.
    • Always have pictures of your spouse and family with you. Layovers and plane rides are perfect opportunities to view the family members you're out there supporting. Plus looking through them on the plane might be a great testimony of your love for family. Also, talking

---

[1] Billy Graham. *Just As I Am: The Autobiography of Billy Graham* (New York: Harper Collins, 1997), p.128.

about your family and sharing pictures of them sends a strong message to others.

- If you are a man or woman of faith, carrying a Bible is a great way to end an awkward conversation. Casually mentioning your faith, the Bible, or your involvement in church also discourages those who might be contemplating flirting with you. Even better, talk about your family worshiping together!

- Call your spouse and family often—at least once a day.

- Tell the individual beside you in the lobby or on the plane how awesome your last family vacation was. It works like a charm.

- Avoid television programs that spark temptations. Even better, just keep the TV off in your room. What goes into your mind will come out eventually. Read a book, plan your next vacation, or—here's a crazy thought—actually get some rest. Viewing questionable material will dull your sensitivity and create impure thoughts that lead to impure desires that lead to destructive behavior. I love the following verses of Scripture because they define this principle so clearly:

"Watch and pray lest ye enter into temptation, the spirit indeed is willing, but the flesh is weak" (Matthew 26:41 NKJV).

"But each one is tempted when he is drawn away by his own desires and enticed. Then, when desire has conceived, it gives birth to sin; and sin, when it is full-grown, brings forth death. Do not be deceived. . ." (James 1:14-16 NKJV).

- Have a glass of wine in the room, not at the bar. In fact, do not go to the bar at all.
- If a meeting is under your control, hold it outside the boundaries of the hotel. When you travel, remember this: you are never alone, and whatever you do in private will eventually come to light.

5. *When at a party or in a group of people...*
   Introduce your spouse as often as possible. Everyone in that room should know unequivocally that he or she is your partner in success.

6. *Travel as a couple whenever possible.*
   If there is any way your spouse can travel with you, even on business trips, do it! I take my wife everywhere I can. When my girls were still in our home, I took the whole family with me on business trips whenever possible. They have always been a large part of any success I have achieved. In fact, they are the reason for most of it.

As a business owner, I have always encouraged my associates to travel with their spouses and families. I'm already paying for their room, their food, and their travel expenses. In most cases, they can take their spouses or families for the cost of their meals. Why wouldn't I want to be a part of their family's success? When their homes are strong, we all win.

7. *Never forget that morals matter!*

Regardless of your personal religious beliefs, morals matter. Our modern society is saturated with sex. One of the factors fueling this fire is the open availability of pornography. What used to be hidden on gas station shelves and wrapped in plastic is now free for any eye of any age to see. It's everywhere—on television, in movies, in music, in print, and, most readily, on the internet.

Nothing is more lethal to your values concerning marriage and family than pornography. As smoking destroys the lungs, viewing pornography destroys the mind. It will inevitably distort your view of what love and sex really are.

Pornography is one of the most threatening menaces to our society. It is powerfully addictive. Many experts agree that overcoming an addiction to pornography is more difficult than breaking a drug or alcohol habit.

Please, put accountability measures in place to protect you and your loved ones from pornography. Set the standard for anyone who enters your home. You can't dabble in this stuff without losing.

Get together with your spouse and ponder some of these questions.

1. Do you and your spouse present a united front to your kids? Do they think of mommy and daddy as a team unit?

_____

_____

_____

_____

2. Do you each have the same definition of commitment? Write your definitions down separately and see if they match up.

    _____

    _____

    _____

    _____

3. List your priorities and make any necessary changes to the order to assure that you and your spouse are selflessly committed to each other first.

    _____

    _____

    _____

    _____

4. Are you still working hard to impress your spouse? When was the last time you did something special for him/her? When was the last time you made a sacrifice for him/her? Write it down. If you can't think of any, I think you know what to do with the lines below.

    _____

    _____

    _____

    _____

5. Do you and your spouse have boundaries set in place for being with the opposite sex outside the home? You've read ours and even though they sound somewhat "over the top"

to some people, they work for us. Discuss with your spouse and write them here.

_____

_____

_____

_____

Life Lesson No. 5

Just Tell the Truth

Let's be real: your kids know you weren't perfect as a child, youth or young adult. And as much as you may think you have them fooled, they are keenly aware of all your current flaws. The fact is, we are all imperfect, and none of us did everything right when we were children, and we are far from perfect as parents.

I am a firm believer in being open and honest with my children. I am fully conscious of the fact that many will disagree with me on this subject. But for me and my house, being completely frank and transparent about my failures has always worked. Not only has it worked, but it has helped forge a bond between my wife and me and our children that still flourishes today.

I spent my teen years in a totally different culture than my kids did. Every generation seems to embrace a new way to raise children, and it's not all bad—just different. My parents were always supportive and loving. My sister and I always had a high level of respect for them. Sometimes it was respect and sometimes it was "fear." My father being a drill sergeant in the army probably had something to do with that. Have you ever dreamed of being in boot camp at the age of ten? I got to live it.

I do believe they were truthful with us, but they didn't really share their past failures with us until later in life, until my sister and I had families of our own. They faced most of their larger challenges in private, although my sister and I were acutely aware when something was going on.

I do believe this lack of transparency was part of their culture. At least we had an open line of communication and were able to discuss almost anything with them. Sadly, many of my close friends didn't have this type of relationship with their parents. Because they couldn't get their questions answered at home, they sought answers from the wrong people, and some of them paid a steep price for it later in life. Either we answer our children's questions, or they'll find an answer somewhere else—one that we have no control over.

It is not an exact science, but I know that hiding things from your children in hopes of protecting them sometimes damages open lines of communication. Andi and I decided that we would rather teach our kids the value of honesty by telling them the truth about everything, as painful as that might be. It was crucial to us that we never give our girls a reason to doubt that we were always truthful with them.

My philosophy is this: if my kids want to know anything about my past, I tell them and so does my wife Andi. Yes, I believe there are appropriate ages to discuss certain topics. But why do we feel that holding back past failures will somehow protect our children and help them grow? It is as if we think that by hiding our children from the truth, we are preventing them from making the same mistakes we did. I'm sympathetic to those who are not proud of their past. Clearly, I'm one of them. But I really believe that children want "real people" for parents. Your gift to them is helping them achieve the standards you wish you would have had at their age. And the best way to do that is to be honest with them and tell them the effect of your bad choices instead of sugar coating them.

Here is an example of how sharing a difficult truth paid off. The question of the day was: "Dad, when you and mommy got married, were you virgins?" Oh man! Any other question but that one, right? My oldest daughter came out with this question somewhere around thirteen or fourteen years of age. I had feared this day would come, and I had dreaded it for years, especially considering my children didn't know I had been married before. Now the question was on the plate and demanded an immediate response.

I could have said something like, "Well sweetie, your mom and I weren't perfect, and we'd love to go back and change some things, but I guess the answer is no. But we truly loved each other and later made it right. We just want more for you and your sister."

How would that have sounded? I think it would have sounded like cheesy excuse to my daughters, just as it would to most teenagers. It would have sounded like I was keeping something from them. Kids want—and deserve—a deeper dive into the truth. They are dealing today with twice the stuff we dealt with when we were young. They deal with more broken home situations than we ever did, not to mention internet porn, rampant promiscuity, reality shows on MTV like *Sixteen and Pregnant,* guns at school and countless other distractions that impact their lives negatively. The truth is, they want the liberty to be real around you and tell you what they're dealing with. And, the truth is, if we are more transparent with them, they will be more transparent with us. Transparency equals integrity. A person of integrity can be trusted. Do your children trust you?

I'd like to pause and clarify my beliefs on virginity. For some parents, this may not be important. But in our house, we believe what the Bible says. Scripture explains that God values sexual purity. Here are some for reference if you'd like to dive into that more: Genesis 2:24; Hebrews 13:4; 1 Thessalonians 4:3–4.

Sex is sacred and should be reserved exclusively for the one you will commit your life to. If you come from a different background and are not a Christ-follower, please allow me to shed some light on that perspective.

We have become dangerously casual about sex. Huge ads with women in lingerie flash even the youngest eyes on mall walls, and commercials with scantily-clad, sexually-depicted women abound on television. When I was young, it was unacceptable for TV shows and movies to portray graphic sex scenes, but now it is completely common and ordinary.

Andi and I believe, on the contrary, that sex is something unique that bonds a husband and wife and communicates unconditional commitment. When children are exposed to sex too early in their lives, they develop a false concept of what adult relationships are supposed to be like. As a result, they enter marriage with a cheapened view of commitment. Andi and I didn't want that for our daughters. We wanted to set a standard in our home that valued purity and abstinence. This meant knowing what our kids were watching and whom they were spending their time with. As parents, it is our job to train up our children, and it is our children's job to apply the lessons we've taught them.

Could I have been able to articulate this thought process early in our marriage? No, definitely not. In fact, there were times when Andi and I both felt somewhat hypocritical since we were asking our children to live a life we had not lived. But we both believed that telling the truth and wanting more for our children would prove to be beneficial in their future.

So back to the question my daughter asked me. Here is how I answered her: "No. Your mom and I weren't virgins when we were married. We didn't start our relationship with honorable intentions. Purity wasn't something we valued at the time."

While we were in full "shock Alyssa" mode, we went ahead and told her about my first marriage and how it ended horribly. I told her how immature and unprepared I was and how much this mistake affected not only me, but her family as well. I also shared how broken I was after the divorce and how immature I was in my next relationships. I explained further that when Andi and I met, we still didn't have our priorities in order. This was a devastating moment for me as I saw myself go from hero to practically zero in the eyes of my daughter in a matter of minutes.

Fortunately for Andi and me, Alyssa was very strong in her faith even as a young girl. And so was our youngest daughter Emily. Emily was three years younger then, so we were a little more careful of how we handled this with her. After I burst the bubble in front of them, what do you think happened? The truth is, not much of anything. I think we scared them straight. Ok, that's probably a stretch. Certainly, it didn't scare them away from talking to us or make them think less of us; this experience only brought us closer. In my opinion, our handling of this discussion indicated that we had become "real parents."

I believe we parents are desperately afraid of approaching our failures with our children, but we should never be driven by fear when we have an opportunity to teach our kids valuable lessons. Every parent has an instinct about age-appropriateness. Sadly, many do not listen to it. Listen to your God-given instincts. They will guide you unfailingly when it is the right time to be completely open and honest with your children.

Research backs me up on the benefits of being honest with your kids. A study of 603 teens and 620 parents done by the Hazelden-Betty Ford Foundation in 2009 discovered that teens want their parents to be honest about past mistakes. Half of the teenagers surveyed reported that they would be less likely to use drugs if their parents would be honest about their past drug use. A parent revealing past mistakes made no significant decline in the teen's perception of them as a role model. And 74% of teens surveyed confessed that their parents were their first source for advice.

That discussion was about ten or eleven years ago. So where do we stand today? Alyssa and Emily both wore rings to display the value they placed on their commitment to purity. We gave them each one of our old wedding bands, and they wore them until their wedding days. The day they put them on is one of the most special memories my wife and I have of their teen years. Actually, while I was writing this book, both of my daughters married the men of their dreams. I could not have better hand-picked either of the boys for my girls. Both of my daughters waited to have sex with their husbands until their wedding night.

Do I believe that the symbol they wore for purity mattered? Do I believe that being truthful with them about my past mattered? Does a relationship of truth and honesty matter to our children? You bet it does. I do know this as well: there are incredible parents that do it all right and still face extreme challenges, but it is incredible to see those kids eventually persevere and flourish because of the love, faith, and standards of excellence their parents sowed in them early on in their lives. I have ultimate faith that when we sow wisdom and honesty into our future, which includes our children, it will pay off.

Being truthful and open with your children secures a relationship for life. Let's remember: kids don't want perfect, they want parents. As my daughters read this chapter, they had some thoughts they wanted to add:

Alyssa's Thoughts

I remember asking my parents this question. When dad answered so quickly, it took me by surprise. I could see the regret in his eyes. It made me realize that my parents were not oblivious to how it feels to be young. For some reason as a teenager you just assume that your parents are out of tune with the struggles you face. They are older, so we think they are far removed from all that we are wrestling with in middle and high school. In many ways this conversation broke down invisible walls. Since they shared something so vulnerable about their past, I felt safe to share whatever I was going through. And I could better receive their discipline when they were honest with me. I knew they set up boundaries for us in hopes of giving us less of a chance to make fools of ourselves. That doesn't mean that I was super excited to be home by 10 pm every night or that I didn't wish I had more freedom, but at least I was clear about their intentions.

I know a lot of teenagers think, "If my parents made mistakes and turned out ok, why shouldn't I be able to 'figure it out' on my own?" As a teenager I watched my friends date countless boys, cry over them, express their dissatisfaction with the outcome of a relationship, only to later say, "it made me who I am." Why not listen to your parents who have already lived through it all and probably know better than we do? On many accounts, I had to face the uncomfortable truth that my parents might ACTUALLY be smarter than me. It was difficult, but I was better for it in the end.

Emily's Thoughts

If all I heard was "Yes, we made mistakes, but we learned from them and don't want you to make mistakes…" A LOAD of questions would have come to mind. The last thing a parent should want is for their children to find answers in a movie, friends, a friend's parents, or worst of all, a boy. The fact that my parents were honest made me feel honest to ask any questions (literally, ANY questions) about anything.

I'm sure it wasn't always easy for them to be honest. I don't know how my father does it, but he has the perfect way of presenting a life-learning lesson in a funny, yet serious manner. Always following up hard truths with his light-hearted humor. I never left a conversation thinking, "Well if my parents can mess up so can I." I left thinking, "I don't want to have to tell these same stories to my children, and I want to learn from the mistakes that they made, not make them myself." A sex talk is about digging deep, knowing the consequences, and in our case, laughing a lot. (Because sex is kind of awkward, ya know?) It was about knowing you don't have to follow a path that everyone else is going down.

1. Did this chapter on transparency and truth-telling challenge or irritate you? Be honest. Right below your initial thoughts.

   _____

   _____

   _____

   _____

2. Whether you agreed completely or partially, please write below one thing that really spoke to you and why.

   _____

   _____

   _____

   _____

3. On a scale from 1-10, 10 being 100% honest, how honest do you feel you are with your children, your spouse or significant other? Does it really matter? Why?

_____

_____

_____

_____

None of us, including myself, get this right all the time. Remember, the truth shouldn't tear an individual down. It should inspire integrity and positive change. I hope you'll be inspired to be honest with those you love. The goal isn't to simply spill all your past sins. But focus more on the change you're wanting to happen in the person you're talking to.

Life Lesson No. 6

Getting a Tattoo with the Family

Ok so maybe not a tattoo. But make it a priority to make lifetime memories with your family. In my case, I just happen to have a permanent memory with each of my family members in the form of a tattoo. Now, maybe you're not a fan of tattoos, and "ink" conjures up a negative image in your mind. I completely understand where you're coming from. But before you write off this chapter, please hear me out: my story may inspire you.

You see, it's not about the tattoo—never was. To be honest with you, the idea of getting a tattoo was something I always considered cringe-worthy. What it *is* about is the power behind having a unique experience with your children and your spouse.

I know there's a judgmental bone in all of us, and sometimes our knee-jerk reaction is to judge on face value instead of using our God-given ability to seek wisdom. I used to be horrible at this, and even today I still have to keep myself in check. I was raised hyper-traditional, and, to this day, still have that *Leave it to Beaver* mindset, but one of the greatest assets we have as baby boomers is the gift of this new generation who won't just say "yes" to status quo. This new generation tests us with their out-of-the-box thinking and their innate ability to communicate in ever-changing formats. This generation is creative and encourages self-expression, and I love their energy and their desire to push new boundaries of communication.

My kids will tell you that I've come a long way, but still have room for much improvement. Today, I still don't agree with a lot of society's "norms," but I don't judge as often. I genuinely try to find out why people do what they do. People love to tell their stories, and kids, believe it or not, will attempt to explain their differences if we just give them a chance.

A couple of these societal "norms" that were my biggest pet peeves in the past were tattoos and kids wearing hats backwards in church. I looked at an individual with a tattoo and immediately thought they must be a thief, gang member, troubled teen, convict, or drug pusher.

Man, is that judgmental or what?

I try hard these days to get to the heart of a person without first forming an opinion. In order to bond and make memories with our children, we must listen to them, embrace our differences, and find common ground. Our willingness to understand them doesn't mean we have to agree, but it shows them that they are being heard. I think this is a HUGE need for kids. They just want to know that their thoughts and opinions are worth hearing. Open and clear communication inspires trust.

So, let's talk about the importance of creating a memory. For our family, it all started on a trip to Costa Rica in 2008. It was our first family trip out of the country and to this day is still our favorite of all the family trips we've taken. We had no idea what was in store for us. The Hilton resort we stayed at was all-inclusive, so there were the obvious perks that gave "vacation" a whole new meaning for all of us.

My kids were fifteen and eighteen years old at the time, and they were thrilled to have their own cabana, even though they crashed in our room most of the time. It also didn't hurt that they could eat their weight in delicious Costa Rican cuisine. All four of us were like kids on a playground. We all experienced our first massages on the beach. My oldest experienced her first taste of tequila (quite by accident), my youngest ate over forty pounds of pizza, and my wife and I felt like honeymooners again.

Throughout the week, we hung together like glue and just celebrated being a family. I was thrilled that we had no cell reception and were all forced to have face-to-face communication. I remember a lot of laughter, zip lines, mud baths, horseback rides, and sunburns.

Now don't get the idea that all of our family vacations took place out of the country or cost lots of money, because they didn't. We've taken day trips to nowhere, spent fifty dollars, and still had an incredible experience together. In fact, some of those trips are the most memorable. We actually once walked into a restaurant, ordered drinks, looked at the extremely pricey menu options, waited for the waiter to leave, and ran back to the parking lot because we were too broke to afford the food. We still talk about that one today and it happened over a decade ago.

The luxuries of the Costa Rica trip were of course memorable, but even more remarkable still were the *people*. They were the most joyful and humble people we'd ever met. Everyone had a smile on their face, and each staff member went out of their way to make our trip spectacular. One resounding phrase we heard over and over again all week long was *pura vida*. The phrase *pura vida* was plastered everywhere and spoken with a genuine heartfelt smile. The phrase means to live a good and pure life. The people certainly embodied this idea. They dressed very simply, lived modestly, had few of the luxuries we do in America, and yet they exuded such joy and contentment. My family embraced the concept and fell in love with the idea of living a life of value and substance. We spoke the words *pura vida* every time we had a chance to do so. In fact, long after the trip was over the phrase still stayed alive, defining the way we perceived life.

We took the trip during our girl's spring break. When we returned back home, Alyssa was finishing up her senior year. She was not at peace about going to college, and neither were we. Everyone warned us that if we encouraged her to take a gap year, she'd never finish college. But, we knew her better than that. She just needed some time to focus, and she wanted to explore some other options before going to college.

I should know this since I barely made it through school. Alyssa at least had good grades. So, against popular belief, we advised Alyssa to take a gap year. That year ended up being a pivotal year for her and was exactly what she needed. Just in case you're wondering, she did eventually get her four-year degree and graduated *Summa Cum Laude*.

The most memorable event during Alyssa's gap year was when she auditioned for *American Idol*. We took the trip to Kentucky in the summer of 2008 and had an amazing time. She made it through several rounds, and we both wanted to commemorate this special time in her life. We had lots of time for one-on-one conversations, and since we had recently returned from Costa Rica, the words *pura vida* were still fresh in our memory. So, with little hesitation, we made a plan to tattoo that memory.

Now this may seem a bit impulsive and unnecessary, but we've never regretted it.

Still... why a tattoo?

First of all: memories matter. Too many people take a half-hearted approach to making memories. Every day and every event in a child's life and an adult's life matters. Good or bad, memories teach us something, and they can change us for the better if we'll just place the value on them that they deserve. Secondly, it was because my oldest daughter wanted one. I knew it for a while and was very much against it. Foolishly, I had assumed all individuals who wore tattoos had some deep-seated problem. I judged without seeking wisdom, as I have done many times in my life. This time it was different. This time it was my daughter wanting one. My daughter—who didn't match any of my preconceived stereotypes for people who had tattoos.

Why in the world would someone want to do this? It's painful. It's sometimes satanic. It's a deal breaker for employment in some cases. Regardless, it just isn't what a good girl does. Honestly, those were my thoughts. I literally hated the thought of it. But it was my last thought that challenged my thinking. A tattoo is permanent;

it's on there for life, and even if you have it removed, it leaves a scar. That thought resonated with me for a full day, and I thought, *Why not go against popular opinion and make a permanent memory with my oldest daughter? Why don't we both get the same tattoo, and in places that wouldn't affect our careers?* So, before you know it, I was on board. I still had reservations about what it would look like and how to explain it to Andi. I knew if I let her get one then I'd have to allow Emily to do it in a few years. As I sit here and write, I don't really remember all the thoughts that went into the decision. I don't remember whose idea it was to go with *pura vida*. All I know is I was getting as excited as my daughter.

For us, these tattoos represented a couple of things. First of all, they are a permanent memory of our favorite family trip to Costa Rica. Every time someone has asked about our tattoos, we've had a story to share—not one of heartache or negativity, but a positive story about our life and our family. It also busted the myth that all people with tattoos are the same. I realized they are not. This opened my eyes to a new generation that sees the world differently than I do, but still cares about morality, integrity, and character. Hopefully I won't judge as harshly now. More importantly, I pray that God allows me to share my experience and my testimony with millions of others.

There are countless ways to commemorate or celebrate a special moment. I could have gotten Alyssa a sweet card, a plaque, a video, or some autographs from the judges, but all of those can go away or be put in a box. The tattoo can't. It's a life memory spelled out in two words. Later, I did this with Andi and Emily, as my original baby-sized tattoo grew with my love for family. Emily got *pura vida* tattooed on her as well, and Andi has a tattoo of daisies as that is her favorite flower that I buy for her often. The more I add from my original two-word tattoo, the more I love it (and for those who are wondering, mine are still "corporately hidden").

An unexpected perk of this experience was that it forced me to rethink some of my other old opinions and prejudices. It challenged my thinking. It helped me connect with a generation I love and want to inspire. It continues to open up conversations with all ages that would've never happened before.

Think about memories that you've made. Were they just from when your kids were little? From when you were little? Has it been awhile since you actively tried to make memories with the people that are special to you? What is holding you back? Life is NOW. You do not get to do it again.

I want you to take some time and think on a few things.

1. What memories are special to you and why?

_____

_____

_____

_____

2. What is stopping you from making new memories with those you love? If you already are, then that's wonderful! Use this space to write some ideas down for the next memory you want to make.

_____

_____

_____

_____

3. What are some preconceived ideas you have about a certain people group? Kids of a certain generation? People who live in a particular area different from you?

    _____

    _____

    _____

    _____

4. How does this hinder you from connecting with them, getting to know them, and being a positive role model for them?

    _____

    _____

    _____

    _____

5. Are your judgments more important to you than the people that they're keeping you from?

    _____

    _____

    _____

    _____

**Here is my challenge for you: Find someone who is extremely different from you. Think about someone of maybe a different age, ethnicity, or lifestyle. Take them to lunch this week. Buy them a coffee. How can you get to know the person underneath the skin?

Life Lesson No. 7

Defining Success

We can have success in business, in relationships, in our garden, and the list goes on and on. But how do we define "success" for a family? If a garden produces good vegetables, it is successful. But in defining success for a family, it can get more complicated. It is more subjective.

I feel this is a crucial topic especially for those who are getting married and/or starting families. If your independent definitions of success don't line up, there could be some very challenging moments in your near future.

It's not that your two definitions of success can't one day merge into one, but as we get older, our "independent" thoughts and opinions become stronger and harder to change. I think this is a major contributor to dysfunctional marriages and families. Whoever coined the phrase "love is blind" is a genius.

Love is first physical, then emotional, and then it grows deeper but, in most cases, not deep enough. We don't often ask the right questions, or maybe we really don't want to know. Absence of knowledge doesn't make the heart grow fonder.

When I met Andi, it was exactly as I told you in the first part of this book. Our relationship started with physical attraction, then moved to emotional bonding, and went deep much later in our relationship. We didn't discuss how many kids we wanted, our unique passions and absolutes in life, our finances, or the differences in our family's cultures. All we knew is that we were in love.

The first few years were tough, not because we didn't *love* each other, but because we didn't *know* each other. We didn't know each other's definition of success. Another way to look at it is, if we do not know our partners' deep desires and what truly brings them joy, we'll never be able to fulfill our role as spouse. You can't help someone achieve a dream if they haven't told you what it is.

It seems strange to me that we spend twelve years or more preparing for a career but only six months to two years on discovering the needs of the person we're about to spend the rest of our lives with. This is foolish, and I know this because I did it. With the staggering statistics of divorce, it's proof that this method doesn't work.

So, let's change the status quo. Let's build better marriages, more fruitful careers, and so forth by knowing ourselves and our spouses on a much deeper level. Let's help our spouses be successful and not just hope the best for them.

I've read countless books on success and gleaned a lot of wisdom, but I'd like to share my favorite quote; "You'll never truly be successful until you've helped someone else be successful." Nothing could be truer.

I believe this with all my heart. I don't *think* this quote is true;

I *know* it is. This concept works in every facet of life from coaches pouring their lives into their players to the mom and dad blowing off a day in the yard to spend time with their child. When we help others be successful—everyone wins. So, what is your definition of success? Is it all about you, or is it focused on others? Your answer to this question will certainly impact your decisions for the rest of your life.

Success is not a personal victory, it's a shared dream.

Some questions for your own personal reflection:

1. What is your definition of success in your career path?

   _____

   _____

   _____

   _____

2. What do you think your spouse or significant other's definition is? Don't ask him or her. Write down what you think it is and then discuss with your partner.

   _____

   _____

   _____

   _____

3. What is your definition of success in the home?

   _____

   _____

   _____

   _____

4. Your spouse/ significant other's definition?

_____

_____

_____

_____

5. Rate on a scale between 1 and 10, 10 being really easy, how difficult it was for you to define success in the areas of your career and home?

_____

_____

_____

_____

6. Rate on a scale between 1 and 10, 10 being really easy, how difficult it was for you to define success in your career and in the home with your spouse or significant other?

_____

_____

_____

_____

7. What steps are you taking to achieve your success? Name one and stay on track.

_____

_____

_____

_____

8. What steps are you taking to help your spouse or significant other achieve their own version of success?

_____

_____

_____

_____

The goal here, is for you to be so innately aware of your definition of success that you can actually achieve what you want to accomplish. You have to know what your spouse wants like the back of your hand in order to be the best teammate to him or her. Know this, no one ever achieved a goal without setting one first. And there's no way to achieve a dream if you've never had one.

Life Lesson No. 8

Just let it go

Why can't we let go of the past? We just hang on to "junk" until we're surrounded by it. Sorry for the lack of a better way of describing this, but that's exactly what it feels like when we can't "let it go." Have you ever felt like this? Are you stuck in regret today? I hope you're not, but if you are, there is a way to move forward. It took me years to figure out how to do this. But when I finally let go, it felt so wonderful and liberating. There's no need to carry baggage on your shoulders you were never meant to carry.

Several weeks ago, I had a deep conversation with my pastor about a few challenges I was having with writing the book and how I just felt it needed a little more content, something that would speak quickly but have a great impact. He said that what he had read of my writing so far was relevant and impactful. It showed my deep commitment to family and that my stories were real-life examples for a real world in need.

I can't describe the inspiration I feel when I spend moments like this with my pastor. He has walked the walk, living a life of integrity in front of our family and our church for over 39 years.

Pastor Ron is not just a friend to me. He is a hero in the faith. As I've said earlier, pastors are not here to raise our children, but they are here to lead, encourage and inspire hope. This is who he is to me.

By the end of our conversation we had touched on everything from fishing to family. Then he made this profound statement, "You know Jeff, dads need to learn how to forgive themselves and move forward. We can sow all we can into our children but they still have a free will. We can do everything right, and still things can go wrong. We hang on too long to our failures but soon forget what we did right. This just makes life miserable. The truth is: just as Jesus forgives us for our sins, we should forgive ourselves for our failures and just move forward."

Well, I've paraphrased the conversation as best as I could, but wow is there some truth to that statement.

I was thinking of these truths one Sunday, when I had to teach our class of young families at church. I came up with this analogy to help illustrate this concept of letting go. I titled it: "Lighten the Load."

My beautiful wife and I love to hike, but neither one of us are in love with the backpack. For those who hike you know what I mean. The heavier the load, the harder it is to get where you want to go. Isn't that just like life?

Andi and I embrace the outdoors with great passion; we just can't get enough of it. We've visited countless state parks, hiked many hidden trails and experienced scenery that simply took our breath away. We hike a lot with our closest friends to make the journey even more memorable. To spend time in nature is, for us, part of living life to the fullest. It's a place where we can leave the worries behind and just be at peace. It's all wonderful until you have to carry that heavy back pack. The truth is that that backpack—the weight of it—and the straps that hold it on your shoulders represents a lot about how we deal with our struggles.

It is a fact that if we carry failures, regrets, financial challenges, anger, and grudges around in that backpack of life, we will never get where God wants us to go. Just as devastating, is when one spouse carries a heavier load than the other, but the other spouse isn't aware. We start taking a solo trip and wonder why the other spouse seems to not care.

Are you *both* packed for the same trip in life? Is your backpack light enough so you can reach your destination? It makes the journey much more enjoyable when we free up our own packs of regret, mistakes, and sadness, and instead focus on sharing the journey with those we love. So why not lighten that load, forgive and forget. As Elsa says in the movie *Frozen*, "Let It GO."

Some questions for you to think about and discuss with your spouse.

1. How full is your pack? Is there anything you need to unload? Name it or them on the lines below. This could be an argument that happened this morning or a break-up from ten years ago. Do you feel a heaviness? Hash out what that could be from on the lines below.

   _____

   _____

   _____

   _____

2. Describe below what it feels like to carry that load around with you. How often do you think about it? How does it affect your day to day? Your conversations? Your ability to accomplish tasks?

_____

_____

_____

_____

3. What's your burden holding you back from? A promotion? Healthy relationships? Jesus? Peace? Sleep? Just name it.

_____

_____

_____

_____

4. How would it feel tomorrow morning if you woke up without it? Describe the feeling. To get out of bed with energy. To be able to trust people again. To walk your path without heaviness.

_____

_____

_____

_____

5. Write down one thing you want to let go of and focus on it. Don't try to tackle everything at one time. You'll be overwhelmed and feel that the task is impossible.

_____

_____

_____

_____

If you can describe it, you can deal with it. I'm not a psychologist, but I am a realist. I know if my hands can hold onto something, they can also let go of it. I realize it's not easy to get over a broken marriage, a wayward child, a bankruptcy, a bad career move, and other traumatic experiences. But I do know there is grace and forgiveness that's available to us. God never intended for us to carry such weight in our pack. He desires for us to take the journey He planned for us to take.

A Dream Realized

In November of 2010, a crazy thought entered my mind. I can't remember where I was or what I was doing, but I thought, "I should write a book." You would have to know me personally to know how outrageous this thought was. I'm a dreamer, a leader, a grower of businesses, a man of faith, imperfect, a man who loves his family, but I am not a writer.

On this day, I fired off an email to my executive administrator and asked her to do some research on how to write a book. I'm sure Chelsea thought I'd lost my mind, but she immediately started providing me with information on how to write a book and how to title it. She encouraged the thought, as Chelsea was no ordinary employee but a dear friend as well. She was my right arm at the time and one of the most talented individuals I'd ever encountered. She knew my passion for my family as did everyone in my organization.

The idea was birthed at this point, but it wasn't until April of 2013 before I put my first thoughts to paper. I started this process at our condo in Destin, Florida. In that three-year period between conception and first writings, I decided it was best for me to pursue life-balance instead of company growth. Difficult as it was to transition out of real estate ownership, this was a game changer for my family and me. I made the decision to sell all of my interest in the company and took the profit to buy our family the condo in Destin. I spent two weeks at the condo writing. I spoke to God a lot, missed my family intensely, but I was able to complete about 70% of the book. My initial writings were driven by my desire to share my family's story and my deep concern over our nation's current plague of absentee fathers.

When I started writing the book, I had been married for twenty-four incredible years. My daughters were nineteen, twenty-two, and I was forty-seven years old with a full head of brown hair.

Over the next five years, life happened. I wrote periodically, but the dream faded a little and the book lost its priority status. During this time, I lost my sweet mother in September of 2015, both of our girls married the men of their dreams, Andi and I gained two sons through the process whom we would have hand-picked for our girls, and later we experienced the joy of our two grandchildren, Olson Thomas Land and Henley Rhode Morgan.

So many times, I have wondered why it's taken me so long to finish the book. But it is crystal clear now: I needed to experience all of this growth to see the true value of a "focused family." I'm a different man today than I was ten years ago, and every experience in life has made me more thankful, more compassionate, and more aware of the value placed on each day God allows me to live on this planet.

Over the years many wonderful individuals have inspired, encouraged, and assisted me in writing this book, and I'm so grateful for all of them. Close friends have assisted me in editing as I need a small army to control and correct my grammar and punctuation. Many have lifted me up in prayer and hold me accountable to the standards I try to live by. My wife is my consistent encourager and inspires me daily. My daughter Emily is the calm voice in my ear that says "Daddy, you can do this." And my oldest daughter Alyssa is the selfless soul who has helped guide this project to completion. She is the wordsmith who can focus the unfocused.

Today, June 11th, 2018, the final chapter is being written, and the project will soon be in the hands of the publisher. I'm more inspired today than I was ten years ago and am acutely aware of the need for this book. Our world has to change, and I'm still committed to being a part of that change. Whether this book reaches the hand of one, or the hands of millions, I've done what I was called to do. I am blessed beyond my wildest imagination. Call me Husband. Call me Father. Call me Pop Pop. I'll answer to all of them.

About the Author

Jeff Harrell is first and foremost, a man who serves Jesus and his family as his number one priority in life. This is Jeff's first attempt in writing, but he sees many more books in his future. Jeff is not an academic, but his simplistic approach towards life and writing has been honed from his ability to seek wisdom from those who have "been there" and "done it"—and done it with excellence. He is a regular guy who sees the potential in others and takes great joy in helping them achieve success. Jeff is a salesman at heart, and he uses that God given talent to further his family's dreams, to promote and further the works of his local church and to help those around him to accomplish their goals.

Jeff resides in Chattanooga, TN with his wife for life Andi of 31 years, his two beautiful and talented daughters Alyssa and Emily, their incredible husbands Joel and Jesse and his two treasures, "grand kids," Olson and Henley. Jeff is a 39-year member of Abbas House Church in Hixson, TN. He is an accomplished singer, an entrepreneur and currently a realtor with the greatest real estate company on the planet, Keller Williams Realty.

He believes there is no family beyond repair and no life without hope. He is surrounded by quality friendships that inspire him daily and he wants to make sure they know how much he cherishes them. And for those children who suffered from family chaos early on in life, he believes a new legacy is possible. He knows that you can never cut down the tree from which you were born, but you can always grow a "new branch."

Printed in the United States
By Bookmasters